How to Get

Credit

After Filing Bankrupcy

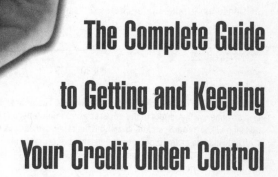

The Complete Guide

to Getting and Keeping

Your Credit Under Control

By Mitch Wakem

HOW TO GET CREDIT AFTER FILING BANKRUPTCY: THE COMPLETE GUIDE TO GETTING AND KEEPING YOUR CREDIT UNDER CONTROL

Copyright © 2007 by Atlantic Publishing Group, Inc.
1405 SW 6th Ave. • Ocala, Florida 34471 • 800-814-1132 • 352-622-1875–Fax
Web site: www.atlantic-pub.com • E-mail: sales@atlantic-pub.com
SAN Number: 268-1250

ISBN-13: 978-1-60138-137-8   ISBN-10: 1-60138-137-9

Library of Congress Cataloging-in-Publication Data

Wakem, Mitch, 1982-
  How to get credit after filing bankruptcy : the complete guide to getting and keeping your credit under control / Mitch Wakem.
     p. cm.
  Includes bibliographical references and index.
  ISBN-13: 978-1-60138-137-8 (alk. paper)
  ISBN-10: 1-60138-137-9 (alk. paper)
  1. Consumer credit--United States. 2. Bankruptcy--United States. I. Title.

  HG3756.U54W335 2008
  332.7'43--dc22
                        2008028009

INTERIOR LAYOUT DESIGN: Vickie Taylor • vtaylor@atlantic-pub.com

Printed in the United States

Printed on Recycled Paper

We recently lost our beloved pet "Bear," who was not only our best and dearest friend but also the "Vice President of Sunshine" here at Atlantic Publishing. He did not receive a salary but worked tirelessly 24 hours a day to please his parents. Bear was a rescue dog that turned around and showered myself, my wife Sherri, his grandparents Jean, Bob and Nancy and every person and animal he met (maybe not rabbits) with friendship and love. He made a lot of people smile every day.

We wanted you to know that a portion of the profits of this book will be donated to The Humane Society of the United States.

–Douglas & Sherri Brown

THE HUMANE SOCIETY
OF THE UNITED STATES ©

The human-animal bond is as old as human history. We cherish our animal companions for their unconditional affection and acceptance. We feel a thrill when we glimpse wild creatures in their natural habitat or in our own backyard.

Unfortunately, the human-animal bond has at times been weakened. Humans have exploited some animal species to the point of extinction.

The Humane Society of the United States makes a difference in the lives of animals here at home and worldwide. The HSUS is dedicated to creating a world where our relationship with animals is guided by compassion. We seek a truly humane society in which animals are respected for their intrinsic value, and where the human-animal bond is strong.

Want to help animals? We have plenty of suggestions. Adopt a pet from a local shelter, join The Humane Society and be a part of our work to help companion animals and wildlife. You will be funding our educational, legislative, investigative and outreach projects in the U.S. and across the globe.

Or perhaps you'd like to make a memorial donation in honor of a pet, friend or relative? You can through our Kindred Spirits program. And if you'd like to contribute in a more structured way, our Planned Giving Office has suggestions about estate planning, annuities, and even gifts of stock that avoid capital gains taxes.

Maybe you have land that you would like to preserve as a lasting habitat for wildlife. Our Wildlife Land Trust can help you. Perhaps the land you want to share is a backyard—that's enough. Our Urban Wildlife Sanctuary Program will show you how to create a habitat for your wild neighbors.

So you see, it's easy to help animals. And The HSUS is here to help.

The Humane Society of the United States
2100 L Street NW
Washington, DC 20037
202-452-1100
www.hsus.org

TABLE OF CONTENTS

INTRODUCTION

Bankruptcy can happen to anyone, from the young entrepreneur to the experienced businessperson. Legally, bankruptcy means that an individual has handed over control of his finances to the court system because he is no longer able to keep up with his debts. The word "bankruptcy" can strike fear in your heart. Psychologists rank it as one of the top five stress-inducing events that can happen to us, along with death of loved one, divorce, disability, and serious illness. Certainly, bankruptcy should be a last resort.

So, you have sadly reached that lasts resort. The most important part here is to for you to not panic. You have many options, not only for now, but also for the future. Bankruptcy is becoming a common event, but because of the high number of bankruptcies, there are many options for you as a consumer. There are a lot of programs designed to help people recover from bankruptcy.

People often go in to panic mode, thinking that they will

never be financially secure again, and that is not the case at all. The truth is, there are many upsides to bankruptcy, and while I do not ever suggest it as a way out, it provides a lot of relief for whatever life-changing event you have suffered. Bankruptcy gives you a chance to start fresh. With anything, there are positive and negative sides to that fresh start, and we are going to talk about all of those in this book — the good stuff and the bad stuff you do not want to hear. But you are going to get the truth, as hard as it might often be to hear.

This book is the result of consultations with some of the top bankruptcy experts across the United States. It presents a step-by-step process to help you rebuild your credit after your bankruptcy. The usual question is always, "Where do I start?" And, while everyone's situation is different, the guidelines given here will put you back on the track for financial success.

Prepare yourself mentally, as that will be the biggest challenge. You do not want this to tear your family apart. Financial issues cause more stress than just about any other life event. You will need to be strong not only for yourself but for your family. Stay positive and realize that if you do things right you will only have to do this once.

This is not an overnight process, and realistically it is not even a one-year-long process. To completely recover from bankruptcy can take up to 10 years. You are going to have to put in a lot of hours, and there will be some serious frustration as you attempt to put your life back together.

Take these small steps toward a long-term financial success. Read the whole book before you start out to rebuild things. You want to know the overall goal here before you start to achieve the little things. So read it from cover to cover, then go back and reference it as you begin your new life.

SECTION 1

BANKRUPTCY
OVERVIEW

WHAT IS BANKRUPTCY?

Before exploring how to rebuild your life and credit after bankruptcy, it is important to know how you got to this point to begin with, in order to help avoid it again. The decision to file for bankruptcy is difficult and complex. You should arrive at this decision after a careful review of all aspects of your financial picture, including legal, monetary, and credit implications. That means you need to have a thorough understanding of the real facts and not base your decision on hearsay or myths.

How Bankruptcy Works

When you file for bankruptcy, you effectively put yourself into the hands of the federal court process for bankruptcy protection. Under this process the court will either eliminate your debts completely or require you to repay some of them. There are two primary types of bankruptcy: Chapter 7 and Chapter 13. Under Chapter 7 bankruptcy, known as "liquidation," you ask the court to wipe out or "liquidate" your debts. This is called discharging your debts. Creditors can no longer press you for payments. Under Chapter 13, you file a plan to repay your debts. This is known as Chapter 13 "reorganization." The plan lays out a process for how you will pay off your debts. You may still be able to eliminate some debts, but you will be required to pay off as many as you can afford, either completely or at least partially.

From the moment you file for bankruptcy, your financial affairs are placed under the control of the bankruptcy court. The court assumes legal control of your property and your debts. You will not be allowed to sell or pay anything unless the court permits it. You will, however, retain control of any property acquired after you file for bankruptcy.

Once the court has assumed control of your finances, it appoints a trustee to deal with your creditors. The trustee is interested in what you own and what you owe. They will determine what assets you are allowed to keep and what assets must be liquidated. The assets you are allowed to keep legally are called exempt assets.

The trustee will go through the paperwork you submit when you file for bankruptcy and will have a meeting, or a hearing, which you must attend, called a creditors' meeting, even though creditors themselves rarely attend. After the meeting, the trustee collects any property that can be taken from you (your nonexempt property) so it can be sold. The trustee will allow you to surrender the value of the property rather than the property itself. You may be able to swap some exempt property for some nonexempt property; in this way, you can attempt to preserve certain assets that would otherwise need to be divided under the terms of the bankruptcy. Sometimes the trustee will "abandon" property that is not very valuable or difficult to dispose of through sales. If the trustee abandons the property, you may end up being able to keep it.

After you file either kind of bankruptcy, the bankruptcy court issues an order to place an "automatic stay" on your debts. The stay prohibits creditors from taking action to collect the debts. This means that creditors cannot legally garnish your wages, empty your bank account, or repossess your car, your house, or any other property. Nor can they cut off your utility service or your welfare benefits.

Even after you file for bankruptcy, there are some kinds of debt that cannot be discharged, and you will continue to owe them even after you file. For example, back child support cannot be eliminated through bankruptcy; you cannot discharge alimony payments or unpaid federal or state and local taxes. The conditions for discharging student loans are very stringent. Under some circumstances they can be discharged if you can demonstrate that you are completely unable to repay them. Creditors can apply to the court for repayment of their debt. If you cannot prove that you are completely unable to repay them, these debts might not be discharged. Lastly, you may not be able to discharge court-related costs.

Following enactment of the original bankruptcy laws in 1978, filing for bankruptcy as a means to escape debt became commonplace. Over the last ten years, the number of bankruptcies filed has doubled. This huge increase provoked the government into drafting new bankruptcy laws to make filing more difficult. The new law went into effect in October 2005. As a result, it is harder to file for bankruptcy than it was before the new law went into effect.

The impact of the new law has been to tighten restrictions on who qualifies for Chapter 7 (liquidation). Conditions for filing Chapter 13 (reorganization) have also been tightened. Below is a summary of the significant impacts of the new bankruptcy law:

- Filers must obtain credit counseling for six months prior to filing for a bankruptcy.

- A person in debt must have the last four consecutive years of tax returns on file prior to filing for bankruptcy.

- A filer must be able to show good reason why the courts should discharge personal debts.

- A Chapter 13 bankruptcy (reorganization) must be paid off within three to five years.

- The result of this law is that more people try to pay off their debts rather than file for bankruptcy.

Bankruptcy will remain on your credit report for ten years. This is an important consideration when deciding whether to file. Bad credit can make it hard to get a car or home loan. If you do qualify for a loan, you are at risk of being subject to very high interest rates until you are able to rebuild your credit. You will also be subject to high fees for missed payments, origin points, and so on. The decision to file for bankruptcy should only be arrived at after talking with credit professionals, financial counselors, and attorneys. There are often other possibilities for consolidating debt and paying down what you owe. Bankruptcy of any kind should always be a last resort.

Chapter 7 Bankruptcy (Liquidation)

Chapter 7 is reserved for those who have absolutely no resources with which to pay off debt. If you file Chapter 7, the court will completely liquidate your assets with the exception of your home, car, and other basic living necessities. Because this is total elimination of your debts, filing Chapter 7 is very difficult. If you plan to file this way you should seek the advice of an attorney.

Chapter 13 Bankruptcy (Reorganization)

Under Chapter 13, you must reorganize your finances and develop a plan to pay off your debts. If you file Chapter 13, you may be allowed to keep some of your assets. To qualify for filing this chapter, you must have some means of regular income. The court will review your plan and set up a repayment schedule, including a determination of how much your payment should be. Filing under Chapter 13 is suited to those people who are in over their heads financially and are experiencing difficulty in keeping up with their payments, but still have some means of income.

Under Chapter 13, payments are reported to the major credit reporting agencies. This means that, if you successfully continue to make payments as prescribed in your plan, your credit score will reflect your payment history and will gradually start to improve.

How Bankruptcy Affects Your Creditors

After an automatic stay goes into effect, creditors can no longer press you to repay debts. However, they may file a bankruptcy petition against a debtor. This is called an "involuntary bankruptcy." If this happens, creditors will review your payment proposal, and they are entitled to attend creditors' meetings and vote on the proposal. The court prioritizes creditor claims and ensures that creditors are paid off as much as possible using all the assets available according to the priorities they decided upon by the court.

After you have filed bankruptcy your name will be filed in the insolvency register. Creditors refer to the insolvency register when determining your credit worthiness. This is why it is difficult to re-establish credit worthiness after filing bankruptcy.

What Happens To Your Property

The bankruptcy court will appoint a trustee to sell off any property that has value and is nonexempt. The proceeds of any sales will be used to pay off creditors in accordance with the payment plan. Payment amounts are determined by evaluating the payment plan, the value of properties you hold, along with your income and expenses. The value of a property is the difference between what is owed on the property and what it will sell for (equity), rather than what you paid for it.

DISCHARGING YOUR DEBTS

Discharge refers to the elimination of a debt. Once you file bankruptcy you are discharged from the legal obligation of paying certain types of debt. Before a debt can be discharged you must surrender any nonexempt assets to the jurisdiction of the bankruptcy court. Certain assets, such as your home, may be exempt from surrender. Proceeds from sales of the assets are used by the courts to settle your debts in accordance with the priorities they determine. After all available monies have been used in debt settlement, your bankruptcy will be discharged. At that point, you can begin to rebuild credit. If this is the first time you have filed bankruptcy, the process usually takes about one year. In some cases, it might be less than one year before you are discharged.

REFILING FOR BANKRUPTCY

You can file Chapter 7 bankruptcy every eight years. You can file for a second Chapter 13 bankruptcy after two years. If you have previously been discharged from a Chapter 7 you must wait at least four years before filing for Chapter 13.

Summary

Bankruptcy can provide relief from a crippling financial situation by discharging many of your debts, and for this reason it can bring you some peace of mind. However, it is still a challenge to overcome. The process of rebuilding credit takes time and patience, and you will encounter obstacles along the way.

Bankruptcy should be looked at as a new beginning to gaining financial control of your life, but it is not a magic formula that will erase all your financial obligations. There are many alternatives that are worth exploring before you make the decision to file for bankruptcy. Many people are able to get out of debt and avoid bankruptcy by careful financial planning and by working with creditors to settle debts or make mutually agreeable arrangements for repayment. However, if you weigh all the options and you feel that bankruptcy is the only real answer for your situation, you need not despair. It is certainly possible to recover if you are willing to do the work it takes.

Frequently Asked Questions

Q. If my credit report reflects the bankruptcy for ten years, will I have to wait ten years before I can get another loan?

A. No, there are several ways to re-establish credit. One is to apply for a prepaid credit card. With this type of credit card, you deposit money on the card, and you can then use it like a debit card. In this way, you can start to rebuild your credit, and you will eventually be able to get loans based on your new credit history.

Q. Will other people know that I have filed bankruptcy?

A. There is no reason for most people to know you have filed bankruptcy; however, it will appear on your credit report for ten years. You can even prevent your current employer from learning about your filing. An exception to that would be if bankruptcy papers needed to be sent to stop a garnishment on your wages.

Q. What are the changes to the bankruptcy laws that people talk about?

A. The original bankruptcy laws, passed in 1978, were revised in 2005. The new legislation requires people to pay off some of their debt if they are able to. These changes aim at preventing abuse of the bankruptcy process.

The new legislation requires that:

- Your family income must be below the state average.

- You must submit last year's tax return with the bankruptcy paperwork.

- You must have lived in the state in which you file for at least two years.

- Child support and alimony must be paid ahead of any other debts.

Q. How will bankruptcy affect my credit?

A. Credit card companies and collection agencies are happy to let you think that you will not qualify for credit for seven to ten years following bankruptcy. This is simply not true. Consider the following: A person filing bankruptcy is already in financial difficulty. It is likely that, before considering bankruptcy, this person has already missed payments and accumulated past due notices and hits to their credit score. They may already have pending lawsuits or judgments. In short, their credit is already affected. Filing bankruptcy can become the first step in repairing their credit.

Bankruptcy will free you from debt and improve your debt-to-income ratio. Debt-to-income ratio is a key factor in qualifying for credit. It can therefore increase you credit score. It helps you start afresh financially and build a new credit rating. An individual filing for bankruptcy who pays his bills on time for two years following a bankruptcy discharge can obtain an "A" credit rating, allowing him to get loans at prime credit rates.

Q. If I file for bankruptcy, will I lose all my property?

A. You will not necessarily lose all your property by filing for bankruptcy. This is possibly one of the biggest misconceptions about bankruptcy. When you file, you can protect a certain amount of property and still eliminate all or some of your debt. Protected property is called exempt assets. Exactly what can become exempt is determined by state as well as federal law. It can therefore vary from state to state.

Q. What happens to my debts?

A. This all depends on the type of debts you have and the chapter you file under. Some debts cannot be eliminated through bankruptcy. These may include student loans, owed taxes, child support, alimony, parking tickets, and debts incurred through fraud. However, many debts are eligible for elimination. Once the paperwork has been processed for your bankruptcy, it is illegal for creditors to continue to press you.

Q. If I file for bankruptcy, can I choose which creditors to list?

A. No. All your creditors must be listed on your bankruptcy petition. Although you can choose which creditors to pay back of your own volition, you must list all of them when you file. Bankruptcy filers sometimes try to keep one credit card active by not listing it. This does not work. Credit card companies generally subscribe to a service that notifies them of newly filed bankruptcy cases. You should not plan to keep any credit cards after your bankruptcy filing.

Q. How long does bankruptcy last?

A. A bankruptcy may be discharged (freed from obligations under the bankruptcy order) after one year. However, that does not mean you are automatically discharged from all of your obligations under the bankruptcy order. It can take from seven to ten years for the bankruptcy record to be removed from your credit report, and you may have a repayment plan under Chapter 13 that lasts for three to five years. In general, it will take about two years before you can qualify for another loan at a normal interest rate. Certain debts, such as those due to fraud, crimes, and fines, may not be discharged by the bankruptcy. Certain other debts, such as alimony, child support, and other debts arising from family proceedings, will only be released if the court agrees.

Discharge releases you from most of the debts owed at the date of the bankruptcy order. Exceptions include debts arising from fraud, certain crimes, and fines. Certain other debts, such as damages, personal injury, or money owed under family proceedings (such as maintenance), will be released only if the court agrees.

If you have been declared bankrupt before — within the last five years — you will not be automatically discharged. You will only be able to apply to the court for a discharge five years after the date of your current bankruptcy order; even then, the court may refuse or delay discharge.

THE TRUTH ABOUT BANKRUPTCY

If you are facing serious debt problems, bankruptcy can offer you a powerful solution. Bankruptcy is an effective tool for eliminating credit card debt — unless you have a "secured" credit card, in which case the creditor may have rights on the property that you used to secure the credit card. Bankruptcy can eliminate any other unsecured debts that you have. Filing Chapter 13 instead of Chapter 7 may put you in a situation where you need to pay back some of those unsecured debts. Once you complete your payment plan on your Chapter 13 bankruptcy, any unsecured debts you have remaining will be discharged.

Bankruptcy is also an effective tool at stopping creditor harassment and collection activity. Once you have filed bankruptcy, creditors are prohibited from trying to collect.

Bankruptcy can also eliminate certain kinds of liens. A lien is a creditor's entitlement to your property that you have used to secure a loan.

Many people believe that bankruptcy is designed to protect both debtors and creditors. Debtors are shielded from acquiring more debt and ruining themselves further, and creditors are shielded from pouring more money into a situation in which they are unlikely to be repaid. However, the idea of bankruptcy as protection is something of a fallacy.

The truth is that, when bankruptcy occurs, both debtors and creditors lose. Debtors lose all their assets, which are converted to cash to pay off owed money. Debtors, who may or may not have entered into bankruptcy willingly, are left feeling an enormous loss of confidence and shame. Some people report that bankruptcy did not really help them. Creditors, too, report that bankruptcy leaves them feeling cheated. When bankruptcy occurs, creditors may be forced to settle for less than the amount owed to them, or nothing at all.

You might ask if neither the debtors nor the creditors are satisfied following bankruptcy, why is it allowed to occur? There are three groups of people who stand to gain from bankruptcy who resist and oppose attempts to change bankruptcy legislation. The first group is the tax collection sector of the government (in other words, the taxman). Remember that bankruptcy does not discharge you from tax debt. The second group is the lawyers who benefit from legal fees, and finally, the trust company administrators who are assigned as trustees responsible for winding up bankrupt estates and redistributing of assets comprise the third group. These three groups form part of an entire economic sector that deals in bankruptcy as a commodity to be traded.

Many people are involved in helping you get out of debt, from attorneys to trustees, to the people who are offering new credit opportunities. All these people belong to the community that is benefiting from bankruptcy. Consider a lawyer who may be advising you to file Chapter 7. This same lawyer — or someone just like him — may also be advising your group of creditors to drop the debt at a loss and take the tax write-off. If a creditor is at risk of not receiving payment because your debts are discharged, taking a write-off might be the best option for not suffering a total loss.

Creditors who are having trouble collecting on a debt may turn over the debt to a subsidiary company for collection. When a debt is turned over to another company for collection, it incurs additional cost and so the size of the debt grows. It may be sold by the subsidiary company to a debt collection company. When a debt is sold in this way, it is sold at the going cost of the debt (remember that is increased from the original debt). This means that it will take even more money to pay off the debt, but note that the original credit company has not lost money on the deal since they sold the debt for their cost. Sometimes debts are sold in this way for twice their original cost, and the original creditor makes a handsome profit on the debt.

Lawyer fees are guaranteed in a bankruptcy case. Tax

agencies are also protected from loss. When you file, your assets are used to discharge these costs first. Administrators take a fixed percentage of the recovered assets, so they too are assured of their share. Funds from your assets are distributed to your creditors after these costs have been taken care of. Certainly, they are not first in line for the distribution of cash.

THE CONSEQUENCES OF BANKRUPTCY

Bankruptcy, as an option to discharge your debts, should always be a last resort because of the impact it has on your credit rating. Let us now examine the various impacts of bankruptcy to help you evaluate your decision. Along with the credit rating ramifications, there are also some legal things to keep in mind.

1. Credit Impacts

From the moment a bankruptcy court order is issued, it becomes a criminal offense to break bankruptcy restrictions. These restrictions affect your ability to obtain credit. For example, if you file Chapter 7, there is a two-year waiting period after your bankruptcy is discharged before you are eligible for a home loan. If you file Chapter 13, you must first pay off all your debts, in accordance with the plan approved by the court, and then begin the two-year waiting period before you can obtain a loan. Furthermore, during the two-year period you must have a steady income from employment and maintain a clean credit record. Any negative entry in your credit record during this period will count against you.

2. Negative Business Impacts

The impact of bankruptcy can extend to your career; it affects more than just your credit report. Persons in bankruptcy are excluded from being company directors and holding certain other positions in the company. If you go back into business, you are obliged to disclose the bankruptcy to those you do business with, even if you were using a different business name.

3. Loss of Assets

Your assets will be turned over to the court for sale and distribution to your creditors. In addition, you will pay a percentage of any income earned to creditors for a period of three years.

4. Family Relationship Impacts

Money is one of the most common reasons for disagreement among married couples and a leading factor in driving many couples to divorce. Bankruptcy can place a tremendous strain on a relationship. Be aware that this might be a problem, and make sure your spouse understands what is happening. This is where you have to be strong; you got into this together and you can get out of it together.

5. Health Impacts

Do not underestimate the stress impacts of a bankruptcy. Psychologically, you may experience loss of confidence in yourself and come to regret your decision. This can have adverse affects on your mental and physical health. As a result, some people experience a phobia of managing their financial affairs going forward. A good financial plan developed before you file can help offset or prevent this impact. Stress can take its toll on your body without you even noticing it until you bottom out. Try not to be overwhelmed by it. Take it in stride — small steps to reach a larger goal.

6. Higher Interest Rates

Be prepared for higher interest rates while you are rebuilding your credit. Your bankruptcy will continue to affect your credit rating and will remain on your credit report for seven to ten years. That does not mean you will not be able to qualify for loans, but creditors will evaluate you as a higher credit risk.

7. Risk of Prosecution

Bankruptcy deals with your debts at the date of the bankruptcy order. After that date, you should manage your finances more carefully. However, if you incur new debts while you are in bankruptcy, this could result in a further bankruptcy order even before you are discharged from the first bankruptcy. If you acquire new debts because of not disclosing your bankruptcy, you could face prosecution.

Summary

Clearly, there is more to evaluate when considering bankruptcy than discharging your debt and rebuilding credit. You should think about all the impacts bankruptcy may have on your life and the lives of your loved ones. This is not to say that you will suffer from all the above effects, but it is worth assessing the probability, for example, of ill health resulting from the stress of the situation. Remember that, to make an informed decision, it is well worth the effort of consulting with financial and legal experts and examining all the alternatives before arriving at the decision to file.

BANKRUPTCY CHAPTERS

So which bankruptcy is right for you? What options do you have? Moreover, what does each of those mean to your rebuilding your financial stability? The first American bankruptcy law was passed in 1800. It was modeled after English bankruptcy laws and effectively created Chapter 7, under which most people got away with writing off their debts. Congress enacted a new bankruptcy law in 1938. One of the changes that came from this new law was the creation of Chapter 13. Under Chapter 13, people in debt would make regular payments to a trustee, and the trustee would pay off the people who were owed money.

Under today's legal system, there are four kinds of bankruptcy proceedings. They are still referred to by the chapter of the federal bankruptcy code that describes them.

Chapter 7

Chapter 7 is a liquidation proceeding. Liquidation means all your nonexempt assets are sold to discharge your debts. The term *nonexempt* refers to assets that are protected by the bankruptcy code. What constitutes an exempt asset versus a nonexempt asset varies from state to state. Briefly, individuals are allowed to keep a small amount of their assets to cover day-to-day living expenses. Depending on the value of their home, they may be allowed to keep their home, or they may need to sell it but keep some of the equity. Assets are turned over to the Chapter 7 trustee, and, after they are sold, the proceeds are distributed to your creditors according to the priorities established by the bankruptcy code. Individuals, married couples, corporations, and partnerships can all file Chapter 7. Individuals filing under this chapter will obtain a discharge from debt within four to six months of filing.

Under this chapter, any wages you earn after you have completed the filing are yours, and your creditors can have no claim on them.

In over 85 percent of Chapter 7 filings there are no assets to liquidate, and therefore nothing is paid to creditors. Chapter 7 is the simplest and quickest form of bankruptcy. It is also the most devastating to both you and your creditors.

How to File for Chapter 7

You begin by filing an official petition for bankruptcy and submit schedules and a statement of financial affairs. These are forms that you will need to complete by listing all your assets and all your debts, along with your recent financial history. Completing these forms can be the most time-consuming part of filing for bankruptcy. You must list all your debts, even those you intend to pay, and those that cannot be discharged, such as child support or

CHAPTER 2: THE TRUTH ABOUT BANKRUPTCY   33

alimony. In addition, you must supply information with respect to your creditors, including an accurate mailing address. You must list all your property, including your home, your car, and all your possessions, and you must list any debts that are secured by that property, such as a home equity loan. The schedules give you the ability to select options for what become your exempt assets. You must be truthful on the schedules because you sign them under penalty of perjury.

You file the schedules with the bankruptcy clerk in the district in which you live or have lived for the greater part of the last 180 days. Your rights, and your creditor's rights, under the bankruptcy code are determined by your status on the day the case is filed.

Chapter 11

Chapter 11 is a reorganization proceeding, similar to Chapter 13. Typically, this chapter is used by corporations or partnerships. Individuals may choose Chapter 11 if their debts exceed the limits set for Chapter 13.

Under Chapter 11, the debtor usually keeps his assets and continues to operate his business. However, his business concerns are subject to the oversight of the court. A committee of creditors is formed, and it has oversight of the debtor's business. In this chapter, the debtor proposes a plan for financial reorganization. The plan specifies repayment details, which may include distribution of future profits and sale of some or all of the company's assets. It may also require a merger or a recapitalization of the company.

Chapter 12

Chapter 12 is also a reorganization filing, much like Chapter 13. Chapter 12 is intended for family farmers, and it has some special provisions that allow farmers to keep their property and pay creditors off using future income rather than current assets.

Chapter 13

This chapter is designed to help individuals who still have income. It is a financial reorganization and repayment plan. It prevents creditors from being able to collect from you during the case, and at the end of the case any remaining (dischargeable) debt is discharged. To file under this chapter, your total unsecured debt cannot exceed $336,900 and secured debt cannot exceed $1,010,650.

Under this chapter, you will keep your property and create a financial plan to pay down your debt over the next three to five years. The plan will outline a regular payment schedule in which your income is paid to a trustee who, in turn, pays the creditors. Repayment amounts can range from 10 to 100 percent, depending on your income and debts. Some courts may rule that you repay nothing on some debts but 100 percent on others, while others will require you to pay 100 percent on all your debts, and some fall in the middle.

To determine if you qualify for Chapter 13 based on income, you must create a monthly budget, which is reviewed by the court-appointed trustee. It will be challenged if it looks unreasonable or if you will not be able to live up to it.

There are some debts under Chapter 13 that can be discharged that you cannot discharge under Chapter 7. This extra protection may provide the opportunity to catch up with debt payments on secure debts and allow you to prevent foreclosure or repossession of property. A debt management plan is imposed on your creditors by the court. Creditors do not get to choose whether to adopt this plan or not. The court will enforce the plan with your creditors. This can be very helpful if you are dealing with uncooperative creditors. The court can also force creditors to stop the accumulation of interest on credit card debt.

In addition, Chapter 13 allows you the time you need to repay debts that cannot be discharged through either Chapter 7 or Chapter 13. Child support and tax payments fall into this category. It allows you time to recover if you have defaulted on your home mortgage, and it provides an opportunity for you to eliminate a lien on an asset that has been used to secure a loan.

Chapter 13 can be a powerful tool in helping you regain control of your financial situation and give you the opportunity for a fresh start.

Who Should File for Chapter 13?

To be eligible to file for Chapter 13 you must be:

- An individual (not a corporation or partnership).

- Have a regular income greater than your reasonable living expenses.

- Have liquidated, unsecured debts not exceeding $336,900 and secured debts not exceeding $1,010,650.

People who choose to file a under this chapter typically meet the following conditions:

- They owe debts that cannot be discharged under Chapter 7.

- They have liens that are larger than the value of the assets used to secure the loan.

- They have more than one year of unfiled taxes.

- They are behind on car or house payments.

- Their assets are worth more than the available exemptions under their state bankruptcy code.

- Their income may trigger an objection to filing Chapter 7.

To qualify for Chapter 13 bankruptcy, you must be making enough money on a regular basis to take care of your basic living expenses and have enough left over to make monthly payments against your debts in the amount determined by the court.

You do not qualify for Chapter 13 bankruptcy if your secured debts exceed $807,750. Home loans and car loans are the most common examples of secured debts. A secured debt is one in which you have pledged collateral. In addition, your unsecured debts cannot exceed $269,250.

With an unsecured debt, you will not lose property if you fail to repay the debt. Credit card debts, medical and legal bills, student loans, back utility bills, and department store charges are examples of unsecured debt.

Debt Repayment Under Chapter 13

The repayment plan does not have to provide for full payment of all debts. It can provide for a partial payment to unsecured creditors. When you file Chapter 13, you are required to take a confirmation test that helps courts figure out how much the plan has to pay to creditors.

The bankruptcy code does require that priority claims be paid in full. The most common priority claims are recent taxes and family support.

Being in Chapter 13 Bankruptcy

It cannot be emphasized enough that when you are in a Chapter 13 bankruptcy, everything you do has to be approved through your bankruptcy trustee. That includes things such as applying for a mortgage, car loans, student loans, and so on.

Once you enter Chapter 13, right after you file the papers, your number-one concern needs to be rebuilding your credit. Begin the recovery process right away, on day one. As part of the paperwork for filing your bankruptcy, you will have entered financial statements and prepared a budget to live on, which takes into account your income, any debt payments you have to make, and general living expenses.

In order to start rebuilding your credit scores, you need to know what they are. You should have copies of your credit report and you should have analyzed them in detail to understand all the areas that you need to work on.

If there is any inaccurate information on there, you must take care of it as early as possible; you want to start out with your records as clean as they can possibly be, so do not waste any time and take the proper steps to get errors removed or place statements in your credit report if you have a dispute.

From now on, you will be managing your credit differently. The most important thing you can do is make your bankruptcy payments on time. This is critical.

If you can, make higher payments than required and try to pay it off early. It will look good on paper, and it will make you feel good. You will get a sense of being back in control instead of out of control.

For the first few months, you do not even want to think about trying to get credit. This is the time to rein in your life style, live within your income, and develop good spending habits. If you cannot afford it, do not buy it. As long as you are making your bankruptcy payments on time, your FICO® scores will be bouncing back.

With respect to mortgages, the Federal Housing Authority (FHA) and Veteran's Association (VA) will allow you to purchase a home while in Chapter 13, as long you have the bankruptcy trustee approval to do so. Many other lenders will not allow you to do so until you are discharged from the bankruptcy, which usually takes around two years.

If you want to be approved for an FHA or VA mortgage, these programs require you to have been in your bankruptcy plan for at least 12 months and made all your trustee payments on time, as well as qualifying with your current income for the mortgage payment. That is perhaps the strangest thing about paying your trustee when you are in Chapter 13 bankruptcy. It actually helps to re-establish your credit score!

COMPARING CHAPTERS 7 AND 13

To help you fully understand the difference between filing Chapter 7 and filing Chapter 13, we will recap some of the major differences.

In Chapter 7 bankruptcy, you ask the bankruptcy court to discharge most of the debts you owe. In exchange for this discharge, the bankruptcy trustee can take any property you own that is not exempt from collection, sell it, and distribute the proceeds to your creditors.

In Chapter 13 bankruptcy, you file a repayment plan with the bankruptcy court to pay back all or a portion of your debts over time. The amount you repay depends on how much you earn, the amount and types of debt you owe, and how much property you own.

You do not lose your property when you file Chapter 13, because you fund your repayment plan through your income. In Chapter 7, you select property you are eligible to keep from a list of state exemptions. Although state exemption laws differ, states typically allow you to keep the following types of property in a Chapter 7 bankruptcy:

- **Equity in your home:** This is called a homestead exemption. Under the bankruptcy code, you can exempt up to $20,200 of equity. Some states have no homestead exemption; others allow debtors to protect all or most of the equity in their home.

- **Insurance:** You can usually keep any cash value in your insurance policies.

- **Retirement plans:** Most retirement benefits are protected in bankruptcy.

- **Personal property:** This includes most household goods, furniture, furnishings, clothing (other than furs), appliances, books, and musical instruments. You may be able to keep jewelry worth up to $1,000 or so. Most states let you keep a vehicle as long as your equity does not exceed several thousand dollars. Many states give you a "wild card" amount of money — often $1,000 or more — that you can apply toward any property.

- **Public benefits:** You will not lose public benefits, such as welfare, Social Security, and unemployment insurance.

- **Tools used on your job:** If your job requires the use of special tools, you will be allowed to keep them up to a value of several thousand dollars.

CAN I CHOOSE?

If you meet the eligibility requirements for both, you can choose the type of bankruptcy that makes the most sense for your situation. However, you may not have a choice.

The new bankruptcy law that went into effect in 2005 set forth the following stipulation:

> *If your family income is higher than the median income for a family the same size as yours, and, after subtracting certain allowed expenses and debt repayments, your disposable income would allow you to pay back some portion of your unsecured debt over a five-year repayment plan, then you will not be allowed to file under Chapter 7. To sum up, if you have enough income to pay back your debts, you will not be allowed to write them off.*

Most people who meet eligibility for Chapter 7 usually choose this option because it allows them to completely write off some portion of their debts. However, if you qualify for both, depending on your situation, Chapter 13 might be a better choice for you even if you qualify for Chapter 7. For example, if you are behind on your mortgage payments but you want to keep your house, you can include your missed payments in your Chapter 13 plan and repay them over time. In Chapter 7, you might be required to sell your house and give the proceeds to the trustee for disbursement, even if some portion of the equity qualifies as an exempt asset.

Your Assets

Your assets fall into two categories: those obtained before discharge of your bankruptcy and those obtained after the discharge.

Assets Obtained Before Discharge

After your bankruptcy is discharged (that means all your debts are either settled or cancelled) it is possible that the trustee will still be holding some of your assets that you had when the bankruptcy began or which you acquired during the period of your bankruptcy prior to discharge. These might include things like an insurance policy, a pension, or an interest in a will or trust fund.

The trustee still controls these assets and can choose to deal with them sometime in the future. Years may pass following your discharge before the trustee deals with these assets. During this time things like the family home and insurance policies may draw the interest of family members, your spouse, or relatives who may come forward wishing to buy these assets. This can sometimes be worked out with the trustee. If this is the case, the family member must make their wishes known to the trustee and find out how much it would cost them to acquire your assets.

If you acquire any new assets after the trustee has completed disposal of your existing assets but before you have been discharged from bankruptcy, you must inform the court of these new assets. It is possible that these will also be sold to pay off your creditors. Also, even after your discharge, you are obligated to continue to work with your trustee in the settlement of your affairs.

Assets Obtained After Discharge

You are usually allowed to keep any assets that you acquire after your bankruptcy has been discharged.

CONVERTING FROM CHAPTER 13 TO CHAPTER 7

It is possible under some special circumstances to convert your bankruptcy from a Chapter 13 to a Chapter 7, thereby giving yourself the opportunity to wipe out more of your debt. This may not be possible, and it may not be right for you even if you meet the conditions. Before you consider converting, you should definitely talk to your attorney and find out from him or her whether this will be worth it for you.

When you change your filing from one chapter of bankruptcy to another it is called a *conversion*. If you convert, it is not filing twice, so you are not having two bankruptcies. You are just changing the terms of your original filing, so you can only do it before your Chapter 13 bankruptcy is dismissed. You cannot convert from a Chapter 13 to a Chapter 7 if you have had an earlier Chapter 7 discharge.

However, even though you are not technically filing twice when you convert your bankruptcy, you will take a new hit on your credit score. Exactly how your conversion will work depends on what court you are filing through, but some will require filings of new schedules and several other types of documentation. There is some work to do to make the conversion possible.

Before making the decision to convert, you should look at your circumstances. How much longer do you have on your Chapter 13 payment plan? If you are near the end, it might be effective for you to convert.

However, if you have a while to go, and you are really having trouble making the monthly payments, or if you do not think you will be able to finish the payment plan because you do not have a high-enough income or sufficient funds available, then it might make sense to take a look at conversion, though you should always be guided by your attorney.

In order to make a smart decision you should also do an analysis on paper of what you will gain and what you will lose by converting; not just the actual money it will cost you, but how it will affect your credit score, your emotional state, and your confidence level. Some people really need to know that they acted with integrity and did all they could to honor their creditors. If this is you, and you will not sleep at night knowing you gave up on payments and had the debts written off, then this may not be the way to go.

When you convert from a Chapter 13 to a Chapter 7, any debt you have acquired following the filing of your Chapter 13 bankruptcy can be written off, along with the debts you are making payments on from your Chapter 13. In addition, money that you have paid out under the Chapter 13 must be returned to you through your trustee.

You can convert from any chapter to another chapter, but you must meet the guidelines for that chapter in order to convert, so you are unlikely to convert from a Chapter 7 to a Chapter 13, because if you met the guidelines for a Chapter 13, you would not have been allowed to file Chapter 7 in the first place. However, there are always exceptional circumstances. Conversion from a Chapter 7 to a Chapter 13 is usually at the direction of the court, whereas conversion from a Chapter 13 to a Chapter 7 is usually initiated by the person who filed in the first place.

Many people convert from Chapter 13 to Chapter 7. In fact, the rate may be as high as one-half to two-thirds of people who file. Under certain circumstances, you can also cancel your original filing and refile under a new chapter, rather than go through the process of conversion. If you do this, you will have to pay new filing fees, and you will lose the automatic stay that prevents the lenders you owe money to from collecting on you. Again, you need to explore all your options with an attorney rather than try to decide for yourself. The law is complex, and if you have already filed one type of bankruptcy, you do not want to make things any worse than they are.

You should also be aware that even though a conversion is technically only one bankruptcy, most lenders will look on it as two. The only lenders that do not look on a conversion as two bankruptcies are mortgage lenders.

In addition, during the conversion from a Chapter 13 to a Chapter 7, you stand to lose assets that you were probably trying to hold. The main advantage of filing Chapter 13 in the first place over a Chapter 7 is that it lets you keep some assets. Are you ready to lose everything?

If you still decide to convert, and you are currently in Chapter 13, then the idea must go through your bankruptcy trustee. In Chapter 13, everything move you make financially is subject to the scrutiny of your bankruptcy trustee. That means that the trustee must approve the conversion and you will have to go through another meeting of the creditors. Every state is different, and there will be varying conditions. This is why you must have your attorney at your side. In fact, it is a good idea to run every financial move through your attorney before you bring it to your bankruptcy trustee just to see if the idea is sound. If your attorney agrees that it is a good idea, he or she may be able to offer you advice for presenting it to your trustee in such a way that the idea is accepted.

No matter whether you decide to convert or not, it is still possible with time and patience and work on your part to recover. Many people have recovered from bankruptcy despite having to go through conversion.

If you convert from a Chapter 13 to a Chapter 7, here are some things that may happen:

- You will have to give all nonexempt property to your trustee.

- Your trustee will sell your property to pay off your creditors.

- You may have to give up your house, vehicles, stamp

or coin collection, any investments, expensive jewelry, antiques, or family heirlooms.

- Your student loans may not be discharged unless they are more than seven years past due, or if repaying them will cause you "undue hardship," which is very difficult to prove.

- Bankruptcy does not prevent the IRS from auditing you.

- You will still have to file tax returns and may have tax assessments due.

- It will prevent the IRS from issuing a lien or seizing property.

- Chapter 13 will be removed from your credit report after seven years but a Chapter 7 may be carried for ten years.

PAYING OFF CHAPTER 13 DEBT WITH YOUR HOME EQUITY

It is possible to use the equity in your home, if there is enough, to pay off your Chapter 13 debt and be discharged earlier. Once all your debts are paid off, you are eligible for discharge, even if it has not been two years since you filed. The advantage to doing so would be to give yourself a fresh start, get rid of your remaining debt, and get to a point where you do not have to go through your bankruptcy trustee to make all your financial moves.

FHA will allow you to refinance up to 95 percent of your home's value. If there is equity in your home, you can refinance the home and pull out the equity (the difference between what you owe and the amount you are refinancing). You can then use the equity to pay off the bills, and you will have a new mortgage under new terms. You must have enough equity for this to be worthwhile, and you must qualify for the FHA loan under the terms we talked about earlier.

Both the VA and the FHA will require you to pay off your Chapter 13 bankruptcy before you get to keep any remaining equity.

Be aware that if you live in Texas, the rules on withdrawing equity are quite different. You would have to sell your home to get the equity, not just refinance it.

There is a nationwide trend toward not allowing filers to pay off a Chapter 13 bankruptcy early, and there are variations on the conditions that change from state to state. Some states will allow you to be discharged within three years if all your debts are met. Others will require you to pay your entire debt, not just the amount that is in the plan, prior to an early discharge.

Once again, your attorney is the best person to talk to about your options. If you think you can eliminate a lot of your debt by drawing equity from your home, and you are prepared to do that, your attorney is the best person to advise you of the conditions that you will be subject to in your state and county.

If it has been less than 12 months since you filed bankruptcy and you have a history of missed payments, there is still another option that you might consider. That is a "nonconforming refinance" option. You can be considered for this even if you have a history of late or missed payments. However, if you have a history of late payments, whether they were prior to your bankruptcy or following your bankruptcy — in other words, to your trustee — you probably will be subject to a higher interest rate. Exactly how much higher your rate will be will depend on the value of your home.

Remember that to qualify for a mortgage while you are in bankruptcy, lenders look at your Chapter 13 payments history, your mortgage payment history and your middle FICO score.

BANKRUPTCY & FAMILY

BANKRUPTCY AND MARRIAGE

Finances are one of the primary reasons that couples argue, and sometimes break up. Bankruptcy will put a strain on even the most solid of marriages. If you are married and filing for bankruptcy, both of your credit scores are going to suffer.

The recovery process should include obtaining credit reports from all three credit-reporting agencies for both yourself and your spouse. Then, if you are going to stay together, you are going to have to work together, as a team, to dig yourselves out of this hole.

When you are married, you and your spouse are technically co-signers on any credit cards and bank accounts that you hold jointly. When you are co-signers on a loan, remember that any impact to credit of one signatory influences the credit of the other signatory. So if your spouse files bankruptcy and your credit is joined in any way, then you are both affected.

Who Files?

You do not both have to file for bankruptcy when you are married. It is possible for just one spouse to file for bankruptcy. However, once that spouse files, and is discharged, debt collectors may be able to turn to the nonbankrupt spouse to collect the debts. You should be working with your attorney to protect your spouse as much as possible during the bankruptcy.

If your spouse is not liable for your debt, then creditors cannot collect from your spouse. Liability can be complicated and can vary depending on what state you live in. Nevertheless, any assets collected after the discharge, by either you or your spouse, or both of you jointly, are protected.

When you are liable for a debt as an individual, the debt can be collected from your earnings or your assets. When you are married in a community property state, and your spouse is liable for debt, you are also liable for the debt, and so your property or your earnings can be seized. Community property can be anything you own from real estate to jewelry, investments, and other money that was acquired during the marriage. It does not include assets that you owned prior to the marriage, and brought into the marriage. Nor does it include gifts and inheritance.

If a creditor is trying to collect your debts from your spouse, check with your attorney and find out exactly what your rights are.

Many times married couples hold all of their financial accounts together and do not have individual accounts.

It is a good idea in general to keep one or two accounts of your own simply for the benefit of building your own credit score. You never know when a disaster such as death, disability, divorce, or bankruptcy might happen, so you should always be prepared.

To be prepared, you both need to have good credit. If you look after your credit scores individually, you can leverage the power of your joint credit.

Leverage

When you are married, you not only suffer from each other's bad credit, you also get to benefit from each other's good credit. If have managed to figure it out so that one of you went bankrupt and the other one did not have to, then one of you is going to have better credit scores than the other.

If you are in bankruptcy, you no longer have borrowing power, but if your spouse did not file, and you have managed to preserve his or her credit score, this could be a serious advantage. Let your spouse use his or her superior borrowing power to get better interest rates and better fee structures.

This might go against the grain a little, especially if you are a man, and you have never depended on your wife for financial leverage. However, it can get you where you need to be, and it is only a temporary arrangement.

You might not want to do this is immediately after your discharge and while you are rebuilding your own personal credit scores. It is important to rebuild your credit worthiness in the end, even if it ends up costing you a little in interest payments along the way.

Remember that you do not get any credit for loan payments made in another person's name, even if you are married to them, but you can always refinance in both your names, once your own personal credit scores have improved sufficiently.

Marrying Into Bankruptcy

You might wonder what will happen to your credit score if you marry someone who filed for bankruptcy sometime in the past, prior to knowing you, or at least prior to marrying you.

When you get married, whatever was on someone's credit report prior to the marriage will not affect your credit scores. Therefore, it is safe to get married to someone who has a bankruptcy on his or her credit report.

The three primary credit-reporting agencies, Equifax, Experian, and Trans Union, maintain credit records on individuals, not on married couples. When bad credit history affects both individuals in the marriage, it is usually a result of being co-signers on a loan or having credit cards in both your names, so it is more a factor of co-signing than it is to do with being married.

Bankruptcy and Divorce

If you have just gone through a divorce, or are going

through a divorce, the issue of who is liable for which debt is particularly complicated.

Once your divorce is final, your property is divided between you and debts in your individual names remain your own, but any debts that you have in your joint name are still the responsibility of you both. If one of you defaults on the payment, both your credit scores suffer.

You need to make sure before the divorce is final is that all joint credit cards, loans, and other debts on which you are both co-signers are eliminated. This includes paying off any tax debts that you might owe on joint tax returns.

Whether married or divorced, you will generally be found liable for a debt that your spouse incurred if you are a co-signer on the application.

You cannot be liable after divorce for any debts that your spouse incurs on credit cards or that you are not a co-signer to.

If you are wrestling with divorce at the same time as your bankruptcy, and you still hold onto joint debts for whatever reason, you can ask your divorce attorney to divide liability for the debts legally, by creating personal liability for the spouse who incurred the debt. If your wife racked up several hundred dollars on your joint credit card or your husband bought season football tickets and you do not want to be responsible for that debt, the absolute best thing is to get your name taken off the account prior to the divorce. However, if that is not possible, you can ask your attorney to have your spouse assigned liability for it.

Closing all your joint accounts prior to getting divorced is the absolute best move to make if you are going through divorce. If you cannot close them, at least get your name off any that you do not want to be associated with, and get your spouse's name off any that you want to keep open.

Closing accounts does incur a hit to your credit score, but it is less of a hit than defaulting on payments and that is especially hard to take if it is not you, but your spouse that defaults. If your divorce decree assigns liability to your former spouse, you may think that is enough. However, if your former spouse defaults and your name is still on the account, your credit will take a hit regardless of what it says in the divorce decree. Your credit card lender does not read the divorce decree before he sends his report to the credit-reporting agency!

Even without bankruptcy, divorce can mean having to make a fresh financial start and sometimes it can mean recovering your credit score. You will have to close accounts, refinance loans, and make sure your names are no longer associated on any financial instruments. If possible, you should establish new accounts in your own name before the divorce is final. That way your credit will already be established before you go out on your own.

You can also transfer balances from jointly held accounts to your individual accounts or your soon-to-be-ex-spouse's individual accounts. That way, once the divorce is final there is no doubt who owns which debt.

Some loans may need to be paid off or refinanced — such

as your home mortgage — in order to get it out of your joint names. You will have to work through these one at a time until they are all taken care of.

If you own a home together, you will want to figure out how it is going to be sold or signed over, prior to the divorce being final. A home is a big-ticket item that you do not want to lose the right to own. Nor do you want to be liable for defaulted mortgage payments if your spouse got the home in the divorce settlement. If you are not getting the house as part of the divorce settlement, make sure it is refinanced and your name taken off the loan.

If you are in bankruptcy and going through a divorce, be sure to talk to your bankruptcy attorney about your divorce. Your divorce attorney may not know all the ins and outs of bankruptcy, any more than your bankruptcy attorney can help with your divorce. Nevertheless, your bankruptcy attorney knows what happens to co-signed accounts, and knows the value of closing them. So give him or her the opportunity to advise you on all your financial matters, and do not keep the fact of the divorce separate from the bankruptcy.

A study by the National Center for Health Statistics indicates that 43 percent of all first marriages end in divorce within 15 years. If your marriage becomes one of the 43 percent, and you have entered into a long-term loan arrangement with your spouse, you will have some financial cleaning up to do if you do not want the joint loan to go on haunting you after your divorce.

If you co-sign on an application, then you are responsible

for the debt no matter who the court assigned liability to, and no matter what private arrangement you had with your ex-spouse. If the other part defaults on the payments, and your name is still on the loan, the creditors will come after you. This may be happening without you even knowing it if you are not regularly checking your credit score.

The only smart move to make if you are co-signed on a loan with an ex-spouse is to pay off the debt, refinance it, or otherwise have it assigned wholly in your spouse's name.

When an Ex-Spouse Files for Bankruptcy

One of the darkest moments in anyone's financial life is when a debt you are not responsible for shows up on your doorstep because you have co-signed a loan. This is particularly distasteful when the person you co-signed with was once your spouse and is now your ex-spouse. The only thing that can make this situation worse is if your spouse is not just defaulting on payments, but goes ahead and files bankruptcy.

When your ex-spouse files bankruptcy, if you hold any credit cards or any joint debt with your ex-spouse, the creditors will come straight to you. If this happens you need to find a good attorney fast, or you may end up needing to file for bankruptcy as well.

Getting Stuck in Collections

If you were not able to attend to all the financial matters properly and you suddenly find yourself embroiled in a collections case because your ex-spouse defaulted or went bankrupt, you should definitely seek legal help.

In the meantime, if you really are liable because you are a co-signer, you can try making a small payment to placate the lender, and negotiate with them not to report the debt or try to collect on it.

Sometimes the only way out is going to be to pay the debt if you want to save your own credit record. If it is a small debt, this might be the easiest course of action. If you do pay off the debt, make sure you also close the account so it cannot happen again.

JOINT CREDIT

When two people, whether they are married or not, apply for a credit card together or apply for a loan together, they are coborrowers or co-signers on the application. There is a difference between applying for joint credit and having your spouse be an authorized user on your credit card.

If one of you has been bankrupt, and now you are applying jointly for a loan, the bankruptcy could affect the interest rate, meaning that payments will be higher. Alternatively, the reverse could happen: the spouse with the higher credit score could help to bring up the average so that the couple qualifies together for a lower interest rate than the bankrupt person could qualify for alone.

How do you find out? You fill out two applications — one each. Then the lender can review both of your credit scores and make a recommendation to you for getting the best rate.

Let us say the recommendation is for your spouse alone to take out the loan in order to qualify for the lowest interest rate. You still have some options. You could wait another six to twelve months for your credit score to improve and then try again. You might decide that it is worth it to you to take out the loan right now, at the higher interest rate, and think about refinancing later on. Or you may decide that you want the lowest interest rate right now no matter what and let your spouse sign for the loan. A fourth option would be to let your spouse sign the note now and then refinance together later on when your scores have bounced back.

Even a small increase in percentage points on a loan as big as a house payment can make a startling difference in how much you pay for the house over time. There is a lot to be said for getting the very best interest rate you can, and if you sense that interest rates are on the rise, and you want to cash in on the lowest possible rate, you may decide just to let your spouse sign for the loan. With the divorce rate as high as it is today, this is a risk you are taking, and you should walk into that with your eyes open.

When you take out any kind of loan it is always a good idea to make sure you have read the fine print and you understand the terms for refinancing. You do not want to walk yourself into a corner where you take a loan out under a certain set of conditions, planning to refinance later, then when the time comes you find out you cannot refinance the loan because of a certain clause in the contract.

UNEQUAL CREDIT SCORES

Let us say that despite your best efforts to choose a spouse worthy of you in every way, they have one tiny failing and that is their credit score. If your spouse's credit score is not as high as yours is, you can help them improve it.

One way is to add them as an authorized user to your credit card account. This is not the same as applying for a joint credit card in both your names. When you add someone as an authorized user, they get their own credit card, with their own name on it, just as though they had applied for it themselves. However, the primary account holder is responsible for the account. You can add anyone as an authorized user, including your children (typically, children need to be 16 to be added as users on your credit card).

When you add an authorized user, credit card companies start to report credit history on both names that hold the credit card. This means that the authorized user "inherits" the credit history for that credit card on their account. Therefore, by making your spouse (or child) an authorized user, you are automatically setting them up with some good credit history (provided you have good scores).

If you are the bankruptcy filer, and your spouse has great credit, you can have your spouse make you an authorized user on their account, to inherit your spouse's good credit history.

If you decide to go this route, your best option is to select a credit card that your spouse has held for a long time and that has no defaulted payments. A credit card with a strong history of on-time payments, with more-than-minimum payments, and no missed or late payments — over the longest possible time — is the best choice.

Trusting the Authorized User

Just like co-signing, making someone an authorized user is giving them free access to your credit history, and opening up the door to a certain amount of risk. However, you do have a little more control than when you simply co-sign on someone's application.

Usually you only get one credit card statement, so you will be able to track all the purchases of your authorized user.

Helping Your Children Establish Credit

We have already talked about one way you can help your children establish credit: by allowing them to be authorized users on your credit card. In today's society, there is a lot of pressure on us to use credit cards, not only because credit card companies push them hard but also because of the trend toward a paperless society, in which we do almost everything with a little plastic card.

More and more, credit card companies target our youth.

The best thing you can do for them is to show by example how to manage their money, and yes, that means managing a credit card too. Budgeting and money management are not taught in school and yet they are critical parts of our life in this country. The only way children are going to learn something they are not specifically taught is by making mistakes. We can help our children make fewer money mistakes by giving them some tools and some lessons in managing their money and their credit score.

As stated before, most credit card companies will allow you to add your children as authorized users on your account when they are 16. In some cases, they might make exceptions.

Do not forget to make sure you are adding them to a credit card with a long-standing history of regular payments above the minimum. You would not want to stick them accidentally with bad credit right off the bat by using a credit card with a history of missed payments. In addition, you will want to find out if the card you authorize them on reports to all three credit-reporting agencies, so that they can establish credit at all three.

You also will want to make sure that the credit card you are using reports accounts for authorized users to the credit-reporting agencies. If they do not report it, you really are not helping your children establish their own credit.

You can start most types of accounts, such as checking, savings, and investment accounts, at any time if you become a co-signer with them. If you do not want to co-sign on their account, they usually need to be 18 before they can open an account in their own name only.

In order to have a checking account, your child must have some income, so if they are old enough to work part-time they can qualify for a checking account and start learning to manage their money and build their credit score.

If your child is a full-time student, most banks and credit unions will allow him to open an account without a job, provided he has some basis of income, such as grants, scholarships, or gifted money.

Do not overwhelm your children with too many accounts or credit cards. One savings account is enough to get them started when they are young. A good time to add them as an authorized user on your credit card is when they start driving (coincidentally around the same age credit card companies will allow you to add them). This not only establishes their credit, but it also helps them out in a pinch if they get stuck on a dark winter night and find themselves low on gas.

If your credit is bad, do not add your children to your accounts. You can wait until they are old enough to qualify for credit by themselves. When they are 18 they will be able to obtain their own credit cards — there is no shortage of credit card companies eager to provide our young adults with instant access to ready credit.

If your children have been authorized users on a credit card in your name, they will have their own FICO credit scores in about six months. Later on, when they are ready to get their own credit cards, they will already have a credit history.

It is a good idea to teach your children not to use the credit cards; just having them will allow them to build good credit. However, these days it is hard for children — as it is for us as adults — to get by without some sort of plastic currency. Show your children your account statement and explain the statement to them. Point out the interest rate and show them how the interest builds up if you do not pay the credit card off right away. Make sure they understand that if you do not pay the credit card off every time you use it, you are paying much more for things because of the accumulating interest.

QUESTIONS TO ASK YOUR CREDIT CARD COMPANY

If you are thinking of adding your child as an authorized user on your account, you can call the companies that issued your current credit cards and find out what their policies are. You will want answers to the following questions:

- Which credit-reporting agencies do you report to?

- Do you report on authorized users or just the primary account holder?

- What is the minimum age for adding my child to this account as an authorized user?

You do not have to use your own credit card to add your child as an authorized user. If you think that it would be a good idea to give your child a credit card in their own name, you can co-sign for them while they are under

18 and then turn the credit card over to them upon their 18th birthday. When you turn it over to them, of course, you need to remove yourself as co-signer.

You will need to make sure that the credit card company you use to obtain the credit card will allow you to withdraw as a co-signatory when the child turns 18. If this is not the case, then you might like to look for another credit card provider.

If you feel your child is not ready to take responsibility for his or her own credit card, you should not withdraw as co-signer. The point is for your son or daughter not just to establish credit, but to develop good habits in learning how to manage it. If this has not happened while they are using your credit card, it is not going to happen when you turn them loose on the world!

Before you make that decision, you should obtain a copy of your child's credit report and teach them how to obtain copies for themselves.

Summary

If your children have had savings accounts for some time, and have been authorized users on your credit card account for two years or so, and have had their own checking accounts and used them responsibly while they have had a part-time job, then by the time your children turn 18 and enter college or go out into the world they should already have solid credit histories and some of the necessary skills for managing their own finances in a reasonable and responsible manner.

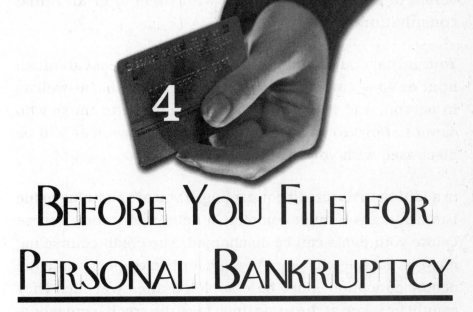

4

BEFORE YOU FILE FOR
PERSONAL BANKRUPTCY

Before you file for bankruptcy, the law now requires you
to get credit counseling from a government-approved
organization within six months prior to filing. The
United States Trustee Program has a Web site that lists
all government-approved organizations. Visit **http://www.
usdoj.gov** and then look up the Trustee Program to find out
more. The Trustee Program supervises bankruptcy cases
for the Department of Justice. Note that the U.S. Trustee
Program does not operate in Alabama or North Carolina.
In these states, court officials, known as bankruptcy
administrators, approve counseling organizations.

Credit counselors with approved organizations are trained
and certified in consumer credit. They will be able to help
you look at your entire financial picture and give you
reliable advice on how to manage your money and develop
your budget. These organizations usually offer workshops
and free educational materials. You can usually arrange a

series of counseling sessions with them after an initial consultation.

Your initial counseling session — which will last about an hour or so — can take place by phone or online, as well as in person, and it is provided free of charge to those who cannot afford to pay. If you can afford to pay, fees will be discussed with you in advance.

In addition to the credit counseling, if you are planning to file bankruptcy you must complete a debtor education course before your debts can be discharged. The credit counseling must be completed before you file for bankruptcy, while the debtor education must be completed after you file. They cannot be taken at the same time. Like the credit counseling, the debtor education course must be given by an approved provider. It will include information on budgeting, managing money, and using credit wisely. It can also be taken by phone, online, or in person. The debtor education will also be provided free if you are unable to pay.

When you complete the counseling, you must file a certificate of completion with the bankruptcy paperwork. You must also file evidence of completion of the debtor education when you have taken that. Only after both these certificates are filed can your debts be discharged.

CHOOSING A CREDIT COUNSELOR

Once you have the list of approved credit counseling organizations for your district, you will be wise to conduct a little research before choosing which one to go to for bankruptcy requirements and advice. The following is a list of questions you can ask to guide you in making your choice:

- What services do you offer?

- Do you offer financial management planning that will help avoid this situation in the future?

- How much do you charge?

- What if I cannot afford to pay?

- What qualifications do your counselors have? Are they accredited or certified by an outside organization? Do they receive training from you?

- Is the information I give you confidential?

- Do you pay your employees a fixed salary or is it dependent upon what services they sell?

CREDITOR'S RIGHTS IN BANKRUPTCY

What happens to the credit card company when your debts are being discharged? All too often, creditors get a bankruptcy notice and they are notified of the terms of your repayment plan. Some of your credit card debts, depending on which chapter you file under, are completely written off. But creditors also have rights under the law.

Creditors in bankruptcy are entitled to:

- A share in any distribution that is made from the bankrupt estate in accordance with the priority of their claim. Most unsecured claims, except for wages, rank low in the priority scheme and often are not paid anything at all.

- Be heard by the court in matters concerning the debtor's plan (in Chapters 11, 12, and 13), the liquidation of the debtor's nonexempt assets, and payments from the assets of the estate.

- Challenge an individual debtor's right to a discharge or to discharge your debt to them.

Following notice of your bankruptcy, credit card companies must stop any collection action, including calling you on the telephone, sending you bills, or pursuing any lawsuits against you. The automatic stay protects you and your property from all forms of collection during the bankruptcy. In Chapter 13, the stay also protects your consumer debts. Credit card companies may file a claim with the court. The notice of the bankruptcy sent by the court clerk tells credit card companies where to file a proof of claim and the deadline for doing so. They must act promptly, since deadlines are strictly enforced in bankruptcy cases. Other kinds of claims on your estate may also be filed by others to whom you owe money. If you have nondischargeable debts (such as those arising from divorce, fraud, willful or malicious acts, or damages due to drunk driving), claimants will probably file an adversary proceeding against you in order to preserve their claim following your discharge.

If their claim is secured by your assets, secured creditors have a lien giving them specific rights to your property. Usually those rights are described in a deed of trust in the case of real property (such as your house) or a security agreement on personal property or a judgment lien. Secured creditors have the best chance of getting relief from the automatic stay or "adequate protection payments" to prevent a decline in the equity available to secure their claim.

If a creditor believes that you are not telling the whole story with respect to your financial affairs, he can consult with the trustee and challenge the estate to uncover any concealed or transferred assets that may help to pay the claim.

Your creditors are entitled to question you under oath about your assets, liabilities, and financial history at the first meeting of creditors or by separately scheduled examinations under Rule 2004 of the Federal Rules of Bankruptcy Procedure.

SUMMARY

Many people have survived bankruptcy and gone on to prosper. Abraham Lincoln himself suffered bankruptcy at one time in his life. Rather than considering bankruptcy a failure, consider it a strategy for financial recovery. After having taken financial risks, it is now time to play it safe. Even though bankruptcy can be initiated by creditors, it is most commonly initiated by those in debt. Debtors realize that they will never be able to pay back what they owe, and bankruptcy gives them a strategy for eliminating debt.

We live in a society in which we are driven to acquire goods, and it is easy to get credit and accumulate personal debt, making it all too easy for debt payments to outweigh our ability to earn the income necessary to keep up. There is also a certain amount of volatility in our economy, so that booming markets and industries can suffer rapid downturns. Businesses such as the housing market, the restaurant business, and technology-related industries are all subject to sudden changes in direction.

Several countries have already developed alternative approaches to resolving the bankruptcy issue outside the normal legal proceedings. Canada, for example, has instituted something called a "Consumer Proposal" that covers debt between five and seventy-five thousand dollars. The United Kingdom has instituted an instrument called an "Individual Voluntary Agreement." Both of these are ways to help individuals deal with overwhelming debt without declaring bankruptcy.

The methodology behind these emerging processes in other countries is largely based on similar principles. Essentially, the individual in debt surrenders control of a large portion of his or her assets to an objective third party and is guided in developing a plan to pay down the debt. These systems save individuals from having to declare bankruptcy, but, in almost all cases, creditors are unlikely to receive all of what is owed to them.

Obviously, entering into bankruptcy proceedings voluntarily is a very difficult activity to go through. However, faced with overwhelming debt and the possibility that your creditors could force bankruptcy proceedings on you, the voluntary act at least gives you, the individual, some measure of control.

SECTION 2

REBUILDING YOUR CREDIT AFTER BANKRUPTCY

Your bankruptcy case has gone through and you are trying to put all this behind you. You want to get a fresh start and not make the same mistakes again in the future. It is time to start thinking about rebuilding your credit.

No matter what caused you to file for bankruptcy, be it from doctor and hospital bills, a divorce, the loss of your job, or perhaps even your own foolishness, you have to start over again. You will need to prove to lenders that you are a good risk. This is going to take some time and effort on your part, but it can be done.

The first question to ask yourself is: Do you really need credit? Life in the United States can be difficult without a credit card. For example, you cannot rent a car or make a hotel reservation without a credit card. The increasing use of debit cards has relieved the need to use credit cards for some things, but there is still a need for credit.

Good credit is essential if you want to buy a vehicle and you do not have enough cash. Or if you ever want to get out of that rental house and own your own home. Building credit after bankruptcy and learning to manage credit after bankruptcy is more important than ever. However, it is also important to realize that you do not need a lot of credit— you just need the right kind. We are not talking about getting a credit card at your local department store. Nor are we talking about applying at the credit card companies that specialize in high-risk applicants. Building credit after bankruptcy requires a serious and detailed plan.

Before you begin the plan, think about your short- and

long-term goals. What do you want to achieve in the next two years? In the next five years? Do you see yourself in a new home five years from now? If so, you should begin to plan for it now. You might be thinking that you will never qualify for a home loan after filing bankruptcy, but this is not so. You will be able to rebuild credit and get that loan if you follow your plan.

By following the steps given in this guide, most people can get their credit back on track within one year. Following the steps takes discipline and patience — characteristics of all successful people. You also have to be prepared to do without some things until you can truly afford them.

It is important to begin the steps to rebuilding your credit as early as you can after bankruptcy. You can begin immediately by making yourself a solid plan for financial recovery. This book will show you how. By setting out a sequence of steps and adhering to your plan, you will be able to get back to a healthy financial status and attain a better life style.

MORTGAGES

The biggest question most people have after bankruptcy is how soon they can qualify for a mortgage. As a rule of thumb, most people can qualify for the same interest rate as people with a good credit rating (an A-1 rating) about two years after the bankruptcy is discharged. It is possible to qualify sooner if you are prepared to settle for a higher interest rate — often 1 percent or greater than the rate being offered to those in good standing. By the time people file for bankruptcy their credit has probably been in a nose-dive for some time. Ironically, after the bankruptcy, people are often in a position to begin rebuilding credit and so the bankruptcy actually helps many people restore their good credit rating and their ability to qualify for a mortgage. By discharging your debts you automatically improve your debt-to-income ratio, an important factor in determining how much of a mortgage you qualify for.

CAR LOANS

You will also receive multiple car loan opportunities while you are in bankruptcy. Just like credit card companies, most auto dealers will be competing for your business. Be wary. Terms and conditions of car loans will vary widely from dealer to dealer. You will need to learn how to read the fine print and understand exactly what you are being asked to pay for your loan. It pays to do your homework and research your loan opportunities at least as carefully as you shop for the car itself. Ultimately, you should be able to find rates and terms that are reasonable. Once you obtain the loan, making timely payments is absolutely essential in establishing yourself on the road to good credit.

CREDIT CARDS

People who have filed bankruptcy are likely targets for numerous offers from credit card companies. These companies know you are anxious to rebuild your credit score and make a fresh start. As you emerge from your discharge — debt free — you are the perfect candidate for a brand-new credit card. Be wise and careful in evaluating credit card offers. Even though you are anxious to re-establish yourself financially, be patient and cautious and exercise good judgment in accepting any of these offers.

CREDIT CARD INSURANCE

Credit card companies offer insurance to cover your monthly payments in the event you lose your income. Be sure you take advantage of this insurance. If something unexpected does occur, any new bills you have accumulated on your credit cards are covered. Do not take any unnecessary chances with your financial future. You do not want to put yourself in the same situation as you did before. The cost of this insurance is very low.

THE CREDIT REPAIR SCAM

You certainly have not failed to notice the growing number of companies that appeal nationally to consumers with poor credit histories. No doubt you have seen the advertisements on television or in the newspaper. I'm sure you have even heard them on the radio, or received some random flier in the mail. And try to think of the last time you did not have an email promising you to change your life and your credit. And then there is the telemarketers, who always call at the wrong time. Their slogans vary but they pitch the same ideas. Here are a few of the most popular ones:

- "Credit problems? No problem!"

- "We can erase your bad credit — 100% guaranteed."

- "Create a new credit identity — legally."

- "We can remove bankruptcies, judgments, liens, and bad loans from your credit file forever!"

Be wary of these kinds of claims. These kinds of statements can lead you right back down the wrong path and end up costing you money. For a fee, they promise to clean up your credit so that you can qualify for a home or auto loan as well as other products. The reality is that most of these companies cannot deliver on that promise they make you. After you invest thousands of dollars into clearing up your past, they are nowhere to be found and you are basically in the same situation you were in before, minus the money you have invested. But there are some companies who are sincere in trying to help you. How do you determine which is which? Here are some guidelines.

THE WARNING SIGNS OF A CREDIT SCAM

Try to avoid companies that show any of these traits:

- A company that wants you to pay a large fee up front before they do anything at all for you.

- A company that does not let you know what you are able to do on your own and your legal rights.

- A company that tells you that you should not contact the credit-reporting agencies on your own.

- A company that suggests you invent a "new" credit identity by applying for an Employer Identification Number to use instead of your Social Security number.

- A company that advises you to dispute all information in your credit report or take any action that seems illegal, like creating a new credit identity. A company should never ask you to break the law.

The law is very clear and you can be charged and prosecuted for fraud if you apply for any type of credit and provide false information. It is a crime to lie on a loan or credit application and to misuse the Employer Identification Number.

Under the Credit Repair Organizations Act, credit repair companies cannot require you to pay until they have completed the services they have promised.

The truth is that everything these credit repair companies offer, you can do yourself. The law allows you to dispute and have the credit agency investigate any inaccurate information on your credit file. And no matter what any company says, no one can legally remove any information that was accurately reported to the credit report, so do not believe the hype.

There is no magic solution to escaping bad credit. It takes a conscious effort, a solid debt repayment plan, and some determination to follow through. The best things you can do for yourself are to arm yourself with the right kind of knowledge, a sound plan, and become familiar with your own credit report.

The Credit Repair Organizations Act

You are protected against credit repair scams under the Credit Repair Organizations Act. The document "Consumer Credit File Rights Under State and Federal Law," published by the Federal Trade Commission, informs you of your rights. The law requires the credit repair company to provide you with a copy of this document before you sign any contract.

The law also requires them to give you a contract that clearly lays out your rights and obligations. It is important to read these documents very closely before signing them. The law provides specific protections for you that limit what credit repair companies can and cannot do. Here is a short list of things they CANNOT do:

- Make false claims about their services

- Charge you for services until they have completed them

- Perform any services until you have signed a written contract and waited three days. During the three-day wait period, you may cancel the contract without owing any fees.

In addition, the contract you sign with the company must clearly specify the following information:

- Payment terms for services, including their total cost

- A description of the services to be performed

- How long it will take to achieve the results promised

- Any guarantees offered

- The company's name and business address

Most states have additional laws and regulations that credit repair companies must follow. If you think you are the victim of a credit repair scam, talk to state law enforcement officials and research the law in your state.

Do not be embarrassed or afraid to report a credit repair company that you believe is ripping you off. Laws are put in place to regulate what these companies do. You have rights; do not let them be abused. Contact your local consumer affairs office or your state attorney general (AG). Go to **http://www.naag.org** for a list of state attorneys general.

CREDIT REPORTS

Your personal credit reports are a record of your history of borrowing money and making payments. They include information such as late payments, missed payments, and bankruptcy. When you apply for loans, lenders use this information to determine whether you are a credit risk.

The first thing to learn about credit reports is the difference between the contents of your credit report and your credit worthiness. These two concepts are not the same thing. A credit report may show that you have conscientiously made every payment on every credit card in a timely manner, but that does not mean you have good credit. If you are making payments on time, but you will never be able to pay off the total credit that you owe, you may not be considered credit-worthy, and you may not qualify for more credit.

A credit report is a history of your credit transactions and payments against them. Under federal law, you are entitled to an accurate history of your credit, including missed payments, delinquencies, and bankruptcies. Note that even after your bankruptcy is discharged, your credit history will continue to reflect discharged creditors who were not paid.

Getting Your Credit Report

Under federal law you are entitled to one free credit report from each of the three main credit-reporting agencies per year. The reports are not automatically sent to you, however; you must apply for them. There is a special Web site that you can access in order to apply for your credit report. This Web site is a central location to access all three reporting agencies, and it is the only authorized Web site from which you should obtain your report. The site is **http://www.annualcreditreport.com**. Another way to get your free report is to call the toll-free number (877) 322-8228. You can also complete the form on the back of the Annual Credit Report Request brochure (found on the Web site) and mail it to: Annual Credit Report Request Service, P.O. Box 105281, Atlanta, GA 30348-5281.

Below are the addresses, Web sites, and important information for the three major credit bureaus.

Experian (**www.experian.com**)
P. O. Box 9595*
Allen, TX 75013-9595
Tel: 888-497-3742

When ordering your credit report from Experian, you should be ready to provide the following information: first, middle, and last name; Social Security number; date of birth; current address; previous addresses for the past three years; and spouse's name. If you are not entitled to a free credit report, they will charge you a fee of around $10 for a copy.

*Note: Experian changes its mailing address periodically, so the mailing address provided should be verified.

Equifax (**www.equifax.com**)
P. O. Box 740241
Atlanta, GA 30374-0241
Tel: 800-685-1111

When ordering your credit report from Equifax, you should be ready to provide the following information: first, middle, and last name; Social Security number; date of birth; current address; previous addresses for the past three years; and spouse's name. If you are not entitled to a free credit report, they may charge you a fee of around $10 for a copy.

Trans Union (**www.transunion.com**)
P. O. Box 1000
Chester, PA 19022
Tel: 800-888-4213

When ordering your credit report from Trans Union, you should be ready to provide the following information: first, middle, and last name; Social Security number; date of birth; current address; previous addresses for the past three years; and spouse's name. If you are not entitled to a free credit report, they may charge you a fee of around $10 for a copy.

Beware of other organizations that offer to send you your credit report free. You are entitled to one free credit report a year from each agency (that is three reports), and the way to obtain them is to go the authorized Web site mentioned above. In the event of a dispute (see disputes below), you may be entitled to more than one free copy. You are always able to purchase copies after you have received your free copy for the year. Over one million people search the Internet for their free credit report per month. That is about 30,000 people per day. Companies offering to provide your credit report for a fee will charge anywhere from $9.95 to $129.95. Some of them trick you into a monthly credit monitoring service. If you use one of these companies, you may find you have signed up for one without realizing it — until it starts costing you money. You then have to call and cancel the service, often after they have already charged their annual fee to your credit card. Do not fall prey to these scams.

Some companies in the credit-monitoring business genuinely provide good service for identity theft protection. If you use a credit monitoring service and want to protect yourself against falling victim to a scam, read the small print in any documents you sign and write down as much information about the company as you can find out, including the phone number, address, Web site, email address, and your account number if they give you one. Many of them offer a free credit report along with a free monitoring subscription period. When the free subscription runs out, they automatically bill you. Some of them will not let you cancel right away. If this happens, be sure to make a note to yourself to call back. It is all part of their scam to get money from you after you put it out of your mind and forget to call back and cancel.

A good service will alert you by email or mail if any changes occur on your credit report, such as address changes, inquiries into your credit history, or new accounts opened in your name. Research the company offering this service before you do business with them.

It is important to check your credit report from time to time. If errors do occur, it is often a long process to clear them up. During the dispute period, more often than not lenders will not approve loans. The best solution is to know what is in your credit report.

READING YOUR REPORT

Once you have obtained your credit report, the next challenge is to decipher what it is saying about your credit history. The next section takes you through the language of your credit report to help you understand it. When you go through the report, be sure to check each piece of information carefully and make sure it is accurate. Even one small error can have an effect on your credit worthiness.

I.D. Section

This section contains information about your identity, including:

- Name

- Current address

- Social Security number

- Date of birth

- Spouse's name (if applicable)

Credit History Section

This is the most important part of the report. It contains a list of your open and paid credit accounts and indicates any late payments reported by your creditors. It is important to check this section as thoroughly as you can. If you find any incorrect or missing information, you should submit a dispute to the credit-reporting agency (see the dispute section below).

The basic format for the credit history section (see sample) is as follows:

- **Company name** — Identifies the company that is reporting the information.

- **Account number** — Lists your account number with the company.

- **Whose account** — Indicates who is responsible for the account and the type of participation you have with the account. Abbreviations may vary depending on the reporting agency, but here are some of the most common:

    I — Individual

U — Undesignated

J — Joint

A — Authorized user

M — Maker

T — Terminated

C — Co-maker/Co-signer

S — Shared

- **Date opened** — This is the month and year you opened the account with the credit grantor.

- **Months reviewed** — Lists the number of months the account history has been reported.

- **Last activity** — Indicates the date of the last activity on the account. This may be the date of your last payment or last charge.

- **High credit** — Represents the highest amount charged or the credit limit. If the account is an installment loan, the original loan amount will be listed.

- **Terms** — For installment loans, the number of installments may be listed or the amount of the monthly payments. For revolving accounts, this column is often left blank.

- **Balance** — Indicates the amount owed on the account at the time it was reported.

- **Past due** — This column lists any amount past due at the time the information was reported.

- **Status** — A combination of letters and numbers are used to indicate the type of account and the timeliness of payment.

  Abbreviations for the type of account are as follows:

  O — Open

  R — Revolving

  I — Installment

  Abbreviations for timeliness of payment vary among agencies. Numbers are used to represent how current you are in your payments. Current or paid as agreed is usually represented by 0 or 1. Larger numbers (up to 9) indicate that an account is past due.

- **Date Reported** — Indicates the last time information on this account was updated by your creditor.

Collection Accounts Section

Any of your accounts that have been referred to collection agencies in the last seven years will appear in this section. It will list the name of the collection agency, the amount you owe, and their contact information. If there is anything in this section you do not recognize and agree with, you should dispute it.

You should also contact the collection agency using the contact information supplied in your report because there is a chance that this is an error in account numbers and the information was never intended for your report. If this does turn out to be what happened, you should get the collection agency to send a correction in writing both to you and to the credit-reporting agency.

On the other hand, you may find out that it really is your account. This could be something you know about or an inadvertent error on your part. It could be that a bill was sent to you and was lost in the mail so you do not even realize that you did not pay it. If the debt really is yours, you will need to pay it as quickly as possible. Again, you should obtain a letter from the collection agency stating that the account has been settled and make sure the credit-reporting agency gets a copy.

Courthouse Records Section

This section may also be referred to as Public Records. The section contains a listing of public-record items — obtained from local, state, and federal courts — that reflect your history of meeting financial obligations, including:

- Bankruptcy records

- Tax liens

- Judgments

- Collection accounts

- Overdue child support (in some states)

- Additional information

    This section contains former addresses and past employers as reported by your creditors.

Inquiry Section

This section lists all inquiries that have been made into your credit report in the last 24 months. Look closely at any names you do not recognize and try to determine why they were looking at your credit report. The credit-reporting agency may be able to help you with more information. Only companies that have received your written authorization are allowed to check your credit history.

How Long Information Stays on Your Report

The length of time information remains in your file varies. Credit and collection accounts will be reported for seven years from the date of the last activity with the original creditor. If you have filed a Chapter 7 or Chapter 11 bankruptcy, this information will be reported for ten years from the date on which you filed. All other courthouse records will be reported for seven years from the date they were filed.

SELF-HELP

The Fair Credit Reporting Act (FCRA) is designed to protect individuals and their credit history by regulating what credit reports agencies are allowed to do. Here are some of your rights under the FCRA:

If a company denies you an application for credit, insurance, or employment, you are entitled to receive a free report if you apply within 60 days of the notification. The notification will provide the name, address, and phone number of the consumer-reporting company that was used.

You are entitled to one free credit report per year if you are unemployed and plan to look for a job within 60 days, if you are on welfare, if you believe your file contains inaccurate information, or if you believe you are the victim of identity theft.

Each of the nationwide consumer reporting companies— Equifax, Experian, and Trans Union — is required to provide you with a free copy of your credit report, at your request, once every 12 months.

These three credit-reporting companies have set up a central Web site, a toll-free telephone number, and a mailing address. You can use any of these methods to order your free annual report.

The Web site is **http://www.annualcreditreport.com**.

The phone number is 1-877-322-8228.

If you wish to obtain your credit report by mail, you must obtain an Annual Credit Report Request from:

http://www.ftc.gov/bcp/edu/resources/docs/fact_act_ request_form.pdf

After completing the form, mail it to:

Annual Credit Report Request Service, P.O. Box 105281, Atlanta, GA 30348-5281.

Do not contact the three nationwide consumer-reporting companies individually. They only provide free annual credit reports through the annualcreditreport.com Web site or through the mailing address.

You are allowed to order your reports from each of the three companies at the same time. For more information, see "Your Access to Free Credit Reports" at **http://www. ftc.gov/bcp/edu/pubs/consumer/credit/cre34.shtm**.

You can order additional copies of your report at any time. Note that if you order more than one a year and you do not fulfill the requirements for a free copy, you may have to pay about $9.50 for additional copies within a 12-month period.

CREDIT REPORT DISPUTES

If you wish to dispute information in your credit report, you can do so for free. You can dispute mistakes or outdated items for free. Under the FCRA, the credit-reporting agency and the party providing information about you are both responsible for fixing errors or incomplete information. If you think you have a dispute, it is wise to contact both the agency and the information provider. (The information provider is your credit card company, department store, mortgage company, or any creditor who may report on a credit application or credit payments.) Under the law, a credit-reporting agency has 30 days to verify the information to ensure that it is correct. If the bureau cannot verify the disputed information, it must be deleted from your credit report.

Step One: Inform the Credit Agency

Send the credit-reporting agency a letter stating what you think is inaccurate. Include copies — not originals — of any documents that provide proof of your statements. Make sure you include your name and address and identify clearly each item you are disputing. Support your claim with a clear explanation of why the disputed item is inaccurate and tell them what action you think should be taken with regard to correcting or removing the disputed item.

It is a good idea to include a copy of your credit report and circle or highlight the item you are disputing. Send your letter by certified mail and request a return receipt from the post office so that you have a record that the letter was both sent and received. Keep a copy of your letter and any documents you included in a safe place.

Sample Letter

Today's Date

Name of Credit Bureau

Mailing Address of Credit Bureau

City, State, ZIP code

Attention: Consumer Relations

I recently requested and received a copy of my credit report from your agency and I would like to dispute the following items:

Item 1: CCC Credit Card account #55555 shows a missed payment. This payment was sent on [date] and was not late. Enclosed is cancelled check #123 showing the payment for $125.

Item 2: ABC Financial Services account #1234. This account was closed on [date] and no money was owed at the time of closing. Please correct the item to reflect that the account is closed.

Sample Letter

In accordance with Section 611 of the Fair Credit Reporting Act, I am requesting that you investigate the above items indicated and delete any inaccurate information from my credit report.

In addition, I am requesting that you provide me with a description of the investigation for my records, along with the name, address, and telephone number of anyone contacted for information.

Finally, if my credit history is updated following your investigation, I request that you send an updated report to me and to anyone who received my report within the last two years for employment purposes and within the last six months for any other purpose.

My full name is: _____

My Social Security # is: _____

My date of birth is: _____

My home phone number is: _____

My address is: _____ (Ave., St., etc.) Apt.: _____

City: _____ State: _____ ZIP Code: _____

Thank you for your prompt attention in this matter.

Sincerely,

Signature: _____

Credit-reporting agencies are required to investigate items in dispute within 30 days if they believe there is a genuine cause for complaint. They are also required to forward any data you provide to support your claim to the organization that reported the item in dispute. Once a dispute has been brought to the attention of the organization, it must review the data and report the results of its findings back to the credit agency. If an error is found by the organization responsible for the inaccuracy, it is obliged to inform all three nationwide credit-reporting agencies so that your information can be corrected in all your credit reports.

Following the completion of the investigation, the credit-reporting agency must provide you the results in writing and a free copy of your updated report. Once the mistake has been corrected, it cannot be put back in your report unless the information provider verifies that the information is accurate. The credit-reporting agency must also send you the name and address of the information provider. It must also send out corrected copies of your report to anyone who has applied for a credit report on you in the last six months, or two years in the case of an employer.

If for any reason the investigation does not result in resolving your dispute, you are entitled to request that the credit-reporting agency insert your personal statement in your credit file providing your explanation about the disputed item. You can then have the credit-reporting agency send out the credit report containing your statement to anyone who has requested your credit history. If you do not win the dispute, you will be expected to pay a fee to do this. Your personal statement will remain in your credit file and will be sent to all future inquirers. You can use this statement to explain information that is in your report even if it is accurate, but for a reason you feel needs to be explained, such as a missed payment due to a death in the family or a lost job.

STEP TWO: INFORM THE CREDIT INFORMATION PROVIDER

The next step in a dispute is to send a letter to the organization that provided the disputed information to the credit-reporting agency. Again, you should include copies (not originals) of supporting documentation, just as you did with the credit-reporting agency. Most credit companies provide an address for disputes — read the fine print on the back of your bill. If the information provider disagrees with your disputed data and notifies the credit-reporting agency that they refute the dispute, they must provide the credit-reporting agency with your dispute notice. If the dispute is resolved in your favor, the information provider may not report the item again.

For more information on disputing credit report errors, refer to the information on the following Web site: **http:// www.ftc.gov/bcp/edu/pubs/consumer/credit/cre21.shtm.**

ACCURATE NEGATIVE INFORMATION

When negative information about your credit history is accurately recorded on your credit report, you have to let time run its course for the information to be removed. Generally, a credit-reporting agency will continue to report negative information for about seven years and bankruptcy information for about ten years. Information about an unpaid judgment against you will also remain on your report for seven years or until the statute of limitations runs out, whichever is longer.

Other things that may be reported on your credit report are criminal convictions, applications for jobs that pay more than $75,000, and applications for life insurance worth more than $15,000. Of course, these last two do not constitute negative information, but all these types of information can remain on your report for seven years from the date the event took place, not the date it was first reported.

Getting New Credit

Having a poor credit report or a low credit score does not mean you will never be able to qualify for credit. Not all creditors evaluate your credit history in the same way; they tend to have their own standards for granting credit. For example, some may only review recent history. If they see that your payment history has improved over time, they may grant you credit despite negative history. If you really need to obtain credit, it may be worthwhile to contact creditors directly and ask them how they assess credit history.

If you lack the discipline to stick to a budget or if you are having trouble creating one to begin with, consider working with a credit counseling organization. The last thing you need after bankruptcy is to watch your bills start to pile up again. Many credit-counseling organizations are nonprofit, and they will work with you to show you how to create and manage a budget. They can also offer you advice on your financial affairs. However, it is important to find one that is reputable. Not all credit-counseling organizations are alike. Just because an organization says that it is "nonprofit" does not mean that the services it offers are free of charge or even legitimate. In fact, some organizations charge high fees or disguise their fees by pressuring you to make "voluntary" contributions you cannot afford.

Many credit counselors offer their services over the Internet or on the telephone. It is best to look for an organization that offers counseling in person. Ask for referrals from friends and family, talk to your bank and credit union representatives, and look out for opportunities at universities, military bases, housing authorities, and branches of the U.S. Cooperative Extension Service. All these may offer nonprofit credit counseling programs.

Financial advisors recommend that you periodically review your credit report even if you have never suffered from poor credit. The information contained in your credit report affects whether or not you qualify for a loan or insurance and can even influence your interest rate. It is a good idea to check whether the information contained in it is correct from time to time so that whenever the need arises to make a major purchase requiring a loan — such as a house or a new car — you are well prepared and in good financial shape.

Another good reason for keeping an eye on your credit report is to detect or prevent identity theft. If anyone has stolen your identity and is abusing your credit or your Social Security number, eventually signs will show up on your credit report. For example, you will see if any new credit cards or accounts have been opened in your name that you were not aware of.

Bankruptcies can remain on your credit file for seven to ten years. Does that mean the information is automatically removed from your credit report after the time has passed? The answer is that it should automatically be removed, but if you want to be certain, you should check. If for any reason it is not removed, there are steps you can take.

The first step you can take is to obtain a current copy of your credit report so that you have the most up-to-date information at hand. Your report will provide you with current information on your creditors. You will need to send information about your bankruptcy to the three major credit-reporting agencies (Experian, Trans Union, and Equifax). Never send original documents — always copies — and keep your original documents along with copies of everything you send to them. Include a copy of your driver's license, Social Security card, bankruptcy discharge notification, and debt schedules. You will also need to include proof of address, such as a current utility bill, that shows both your name and your address. Include a letter stating that it has been ten years since the bankruptcy, and you would like the information cleared from your record.

Allow 30 days for the agencies to process this information, plus five or so days for mailing. After 35 days, obtain another copy of your credit report and see how it looks. Do not forget that you will have to obtain separate copies from each of the three agencies. When everything is in order, debts from the bankruptcy should show a $0 balance and nothing about the bankruptcy should appear on the report.

Bankruptcy allows you to wipe your slate clean and make a fresh financial start. It is important to learn from these lessons and not repeat them in the future. Use the advice you have received during your bankruptcy process to plan and budget so that history does not repeat itself.

SECTION 3

HAVE A PLAN

YOUR PLAN

For most people the main goal in life is to be happy and successful. Often the two go hand in hand. In today's society, many of us define ourselves by what we own. For some, financial success is a huge force that causes them to neglect their marriage, their children, and their health. For others, it is worth the risk of entering into illegal dealings.

Even when people are financially successful, that sometimes is not enough. In addition, they feel the need to show the world how successful they are by buying expensive homes, cars, clothes, and so forth. Some people try to project a successful image by adopting a life style they cannot afford with their current income. However, whether people are really successful, or just successfully projecting a life style image, disaster can strike at any time. We become ill, we have accidents, we lose jobs, and so on. Situations like this can drain us financially and leave us unable to cope with additional expenses. Why is it that some people are able to overcome adversities such as these circumstances while others are not? The difference is in how prepared you are.

During your bankruptcy you will go through financial planning and be required to come up with a payment plan to manage your debts and a budget. At the end of the bankruptcy, when your bills have been discharged, it is a good idea to continue with financial planning and budgeting. You can look at your bankruptcy as a tool that helped you get back on track financially and that helped you learn from your experiences. By now you have a good feel for how your spending habits caused you to end up in bankruptcy court, and you know you have to do better to avoid being in the same situation in the future. Hopefully it is not an experience you would want to go through a second time. Whether your bankruptcy was the result of poorly executed business practices or poorly managed personal accounting, a good plan, together with everything you have learned, will help keep you in the black in the future.

Here is some practical advice you can apply to get your life back on track as soon as possible and return to a way of life free from financial worry:

1. Seek moral support. It is surprising how many people will not understand what you experienced by going through bankruptcy. Depend on your immediate and close friends for moral support during this difficult time and to keep you encouraged as you implement your financial recovery plan. Stay away from negative people who are not supporting you in your situation or from whom you may have received bad advice in the past. Look for positive people and anyone who can give you real help to get back on your feet.

2. **Be responsible with money.** This means that you should be really responsible. You can blame your inability to afford things you want on the cost of living, a misguided business partner, or a falling stock market. Now that you know how easy it is to get in over your head, you need to take a critical look at your spending habits. Consider all the things you have purchased in the past that you really could not afford. Did you really need those things or did you just want them? Think about things you may have paid dearly for on your credit card that you really did not get a lot of use out of, and ways in which you probably wasted money.

3. **Get paying work immediately.** Become productive and earn money as quickly as you possibly can. Explore every avenue and every opportunity for employment. Make a list of all the things you are qualified to do and all the potential contacts you could network with. There are numerous Web sites that will email you every week with job listings. If you are having trouble finding work, do not hold out for that ultimate job; take whatever you can get and keep on looking. At least you will be gaining experience and making money while you continue to search for a better fit.

4. **Join a credit union.** Credit unions can offer loans which banks might not offer you. If you are already a member of a credit union, when it is time to apply for a major loan your application will stand a better chance of being accepted.

5. Save money. Most people do not have a good plan for their retirement even though they realize how important it is. Find a good financial advisor who can make recommendations in line with your life style and income. Begin to set aside cash reserves to protect your family against emergencies and avoid high-risk investment schemes. You should also look into insurance to protect your family and your remaining assets.

6. Keep records. Track all spending, especially debts owed and amounts paid to your creditors. Record other spending and analyze your spending habits. This will give you insights into where you can save money, let you know how much you really spend on things like pizza and entertainment, and it will help you determine where you can make cutbacks to find additional ways to pay off your debts and increase your savings.

7. Get smart about money. Robert Kiyosaki, author of *Rich Dad, Poor Dad*, is a strong advocate for personal financial education. Read, read, read. You can find plenty of information, guidance, and self-help literature in your local library. Learn how others, especially wealthy people, think about money, and you will begin to develop your own strategies for financial success.

8. Create a plan: Look at where you have been and where you want to be financially and decide what is possible with your income. How much do you need for basic living expenses? How much can

you afford to save? How much are you spending to pay down your debt? How much can you afford to spend on luxury items or entertainment? By keeping a monthly budget, even a simple recording of everything you earn and everything you spend, you will begin to develop a much better sense of what you can really afford.

9. Be selective: Be selective about the money you borrow. Do not buy things you do not need on credit. You end up paying much more than they are worth. Instead, save up cash for items you want but do not need.

10. Get a secured credit card: Secured credit cards allow you to deposit money on a credit card and then use the credit card to spend that much money. This is a good approach for relearning how to manage your credit card, and it allows you to rebuild your credit safely, while slowly proving to the credit bureaus and future lenders that you can be a good credit risk. A simple strategy for rebuilding credit is to get a credit card to use at your local gas station or grocery store. Then begin using it instead of paying cash, but set the cash aside and pay the credit card off religiously every month. By making small, manageable charges every month that you know you can pay off, you can use a credit card without carrying a balance. This shows lenders that they can trust you with a credit card. As you master this approach, you can slowly begin to build up the amounts you charge and pay them off in two months instead of one. Never make the minimum payment on a credit card. Minimum payments are developed to drag your loan out for

as long as possible and make you pay interest over many months.

11. Use credit companies that report to the credit reporting agencies. Some companies do not report to the credit-reporting agencies so your on-time payments are doing nothing to help your credit scores. Ask first, and then work with companies that will help you increase your credit score by reporting them.

12. Pay all your bills on time.

After following these steps for several months, you will be in a position to finance a new car or home within a couple of years. As the saying goes, "Time heals all wounds." It will take years to be a "normal" person again, but once you know you have attained the discipline to practice good habits, there is no reason you should fall back into your old habits. As you become wiser, you can better inform others about the unhealthy influences of commercialism and consumerism.

MAKE A FRESH START MENTALLY

Bankruptcy can be stressful and discouraging, while simultaneously being a freeing experience for millions of Americans every year. Depending on which type of bankruptcy you file, you are either relieved of all of your debt through the liquidation of your assets or you may be making monitored payments to your debtors.

This may prove to be quite beneficial. Your financial life

is finally under control. However, because bankruptcy is perhaps the worst mark that can appear on one's credit, you may find yourself feeling depressed or discouraged. You must not only focus on rebuilding your credit but also your self-esteem. Think of this experience as an opportunity for a fresh start in your life and stay on track with your plan. As you follow your plan and see your finances begin to take new shape, you will find encouragement from even small successes, so stay positive, and you may find that life can be so much better than before your bankruptcy.

People who have recovered from bankruptcy do not usually live in poverty. Some of them go on to be rich and financially healthy. Most end up with credit scores well above what they experienced before the bankruptcy, and most people find their way back to buying homes, cars, and all the other things we like to have in our lives.

CHOOSING A LOAN

When comparing the rates of the loans from various lenders, become knowledgeable about interest rates. You should understand what the current prime interest is, since many loans have interest rates that are tied to the prime rate. That means if the prime interest rate goes up or down, so does the interest rate you pay on your loan. Credit cards' interest rates are typically well above prime, but if you shop around you will find that interest rates on credit cards can vary quite a bit.

You also need to be aware of the difference between the annual percentage rate (APR) and the interest rate. The

APR gives you the true value of what you are paying for the loan. The APR includes the fees, as well as the interest rate charged on the loan. When you are shopping for a loan, ask about the APR, and ask what fees you are being charged for the loan. Be aware that there may be maintenance fees charged periodically, as well as up-front closing costs. Read the fine print and be sure you understand exactly what you are agreeing to when you accept a loan. Do careful comparisons of several different loans before you decide to sign your name on the dotted line.

Before you get serious about taking out a loan and do your research to find the best terms, you should also seriously consider whether you can afford to make payments. Review your budget, take a good look at where you stand with respect to any prebankruptcy debts that you are managing, and ask yourself if you honestly need to borrow money at this point in your life. No matter what, you must be prompt at making payments on any existing or new debts.

Master List

If you have never budgeted before, it can be daunting to figure out how to develop your plan and what you should keep track of. The simple answer is everything. Every penny spent and every penny earned should be accounted for in your budget. You can begin by developing a spreadsheet to manage your credit card payments.

A spreadsheet allows you to input all credit card and loan information so you can quickly and easily see which credit card accounts you need to pay off or pay down to increase your credit score and reduce your debt. You can use a computer program to build your spreadsheet or you can do it the old-fashioned way using some paper and a pen.

When you create the spreadsheet, you should include information about your credit cards, such as the interest rates, credit limit, and the customer service number. If your credit cards are lost or stolen, you will have all the information in one place so you can act fast to protect your personal credit reports. Knowing what interest rates you are paying on each loan will help you decide which ones to pay down first. Pay down the highest interest rate first. If you do have to use a credit card to make a purchase, use the one with the lowest interest rate. If you are adding credit account information to the spreadsheet, be sure to keep it in a safe place.

Keeping the list updated each month will give you an accurate picture of your total debt and an idea of how well you are managing it.

Here is the information you should track on your spreadsheet:

- Lender

- Phone number

- Account number

- Annual percentage rate (APR)

- Account balances

- Credit limit

- Due date

- Amount of last payment

Optionally you can record how much interest is calculated on each statement. Tracking the amount you are paying in interest alone is a powerful incentive for keeping your credit card at home and saving up to pay cash for items you need.

Employment

Many companies are now checking your credit report and using it as part of the interview process. If you have ever applied for a job that you were sure you would get and then been turned down, maybe your credit report is the reason. However, the law does offer you protection against being turned down for a job based upon a bankruptcy. There are rules governing how employers can and cannot use the information they find in your credit report to make hiring decisions.

It has been standard practice for some time for employers in certain industry sectors, such as the financial and gaming sectors and in government, to screen employees' credit records. However, the practice is becoming more widespread in other industries as well.

Recently, pre-employment screening agencies have noticed a surge in requests for full background checks, which can investigate credit reports, as well as criminal records, driving records, and employment and education history.

It is thought that between 50 and 70 percent of all companies currently review personal credit reports, giving them access to your personal financial information, including bankruptcies, liens, judgments, and loan and credit card payment history. Employers use this information to try to understand whether a potential employee will be a security risk, subject to bribery, and willing to give unauthorized individuals access to company information. The bottom line is that some employers believe that bad credit scores are an indication of being irresponsible and showing little regard for confidential company information.

Dealing With Employment Credit Checks

First, the bankruptcy code prohibits employers from discriminating against applicants based solely on a bankruptcy reported on your credit report. Second, you are not obligated to tell your employer, or future employer, if you are going through bankruptcy or have gone through it in the past. This holds true whether you are applying for a new position or for a promotion.

If you are applying for a new job after filing bankruptcy and you suspect that your employer may run a credit report on you and discover the information, there are some strategies you can use to safeguard yourself.

First, if you know that this employer will be running a credit check, be up front and honest about your bankruptcy. Describe in simple terms what caused it and indicate that you are on the road to financial recovery. Honesty is a powerful tool.

If, on the other hand, you are not sure whether the employer will run a credit check, do not tell your potential employer right up front about the bankruptcy. Wait and see if there is a second or third interview. Once you sense that an offer is imminent, you can disclose the bankruptcy.

Be matter-of-fact and straightforward about disclosing your bankruptcy and do not go into a lot of gory detail. Let employers know that you are in control of your financial responsibilities and back on the right path. A bankruptcy is not always caused by financial irresponsibility. Do not underestimate a potential employer's ability to understand your situation.

Your Rights Regarding Employment Credit Checks

As with most things, when it comes to credit checks, knowledge is your best weapon. It pays to know and understand your rights. The Fair Credit Reporting Act provides protection for you under the law. Sections 604, 606, and 615 of this act regulate what employers can do with respect to credit report checks.

An employer must notify you in writing that your credit rating score may be used in the job evaluation and obtain your written authorization before running a check on your credit reports. But remember, sometimes the employer will "notify" you in the fine print. In other words, they will "tell" you without really "telling" you. So make sure you always read the fine print on the forms the human resources person hands you during the interview.

If your employer, or potential employer, sees something

on your personal credit reports that may cause them not to hire you, or to fire you, they must send you a "Pre-Adverse Action Disclosure." The Pre-Adverse Action Disclosure forewarns you what the employer has found going against you and provides you with an opportunity to offer a mitigating explanation or to fix the information if it is an error. However, the burden is on you to act fast. The notice will contain contact information for the credit-reporting agency that supplied the information to your employer. It will specify that you have the right to dispute the information and the right to request an additional free report within 60 days.

BANKRUPTCY DISCRIMINATION

While employers can legally terminate or deny a job or promotion to those with bad credit, Section 525 of the U.S. Bankruptcy Code prohibits discrimination based solely on bankruptcy. Proving discrimination is never easy. If the bankruptcy is the only negative item on your credit report, you might have some chance in a discrimination lawsuit. If there are other negative items, though, it may be very hard to win.

The truth is, if an employer does not want to hire you because of the bankruptcy on your credit reports, it is easy for them to claim they did not hire you for another reason. But if an employer actually offers you the job and rescinds it after running a background check, and the background check shows all high marks except the bankruptcy, your chances of mounting a successful case increase.

Bottom line: If the ONLY negative item on your credit

report is a bankruptcy, you have a better chance of getting the job than you do if you have many other negative items on your credit reports.

Employment credit checks are one reason it is so important to make sure you get copies of all three of your credit reports. Review them carefully, and if there are any inaccurate, incomplete, misleading, unverifiable, or outdated items on your reports, get them taken off. If you are running into difficulties with your disputes, we recommend you use an attorney who specializes in credit law. It will cost you money, but if it is preventing you from being hired, the results could be well worth it.

To sum up, when you are trying to be hired, here is a short list of things to remember:

1. Always read the fine print before you sign anything.

2. Determine the right strategy for revealing your bankruptcy to your potential employer.

3. Regularly check your credit reports so you are sure that nothing is on there that should not be.

4. If your employer sends you a Pre-Adverse Action Disclosure, know your rights.

5. Hire an attorney to dispute anything on your reports that appears to be inaccurate, incomplete, misleading, unverifiable, or outdated.

SECTION 4

CREDIT CARD APPLICATIONS

APPLYING FOR CREDIT CARDS

For many of us, credit cards are the reason we filed bankruptcy in the first place. And a mistake many people make after filing bankruptcy is to avoid using credit altogether. The fact of the matter is, if you want to re-establish your credit and start to get approved for mainstream loans at low interest rates, you must have a credit card or two. The trick is to use them wisely.

If you have been trying to open a new credit card, but keep being denied every time you apply, this section will help you understand how to fill out the credit card application in such a way that it will be approved and how you can obtain the best interest rates — even if you have filed for bankruptcy.

Filling out the application properly is very important. It is amazing how many people are denied credit simply because they do not take sufficient care with the details of the application form.

Here are a few rules to follow.

GATHER YOUR DOCUMENTATION

The first step to properly completing any credit application begins with assembling all your information. You should keep all your important information in a single folder so that when you need to supply some information about yourself or your bankruptcy it is easy to find.

In the credit folder you will want to put all the following pieces of information:

- Your bankruptcy discharge letter

- A recent copy of your credit report from all three credit-reporting agencies

- A copy of your complete bankruptcy petition

- Copies of all credit applications and established credit accounts since your bankruptcy

- Facts about you, your spouse — if applicable — and your nearest relative. Include dates of birth, Social Security numbers, your address and telephone number, driver's license number, salary, employer, employer's address and telephone number, and any other information you think may be important.

- A short letter explaining about why you filed for bankruptcy

A credit folder will ensure that you can easily find information so that you do not leave any blank spaces on the credit application. Every time you fill out a credit application you need information like your parents' address, your nearest relative's telephone number, your spouse's Social Security Number, bank account numbers, previous addresses, employers' addresses, dates of employment, birthdays, driver's license numbers, or any of the other information you might not usually use on a daily basis.

Keep the credit folder in a safe place. It is now loaded with personal information about your identity.

Having all the vital information you need in one place will allow you to complete each credit application completely and consistently.

ALWAYS COMPLETE THE CREDIT APPLICATION AT HOME

You do not want to carry around your credit folder containing all your important personal information. But that is not the only reason you should complete credit applications at home. You do not want to feel rushed or intimidated into filling out a credit application on the spot. Take the application with you. Fill it out in its entirety at home where you can think clearly and consult your facts. Then fax, mail, or drop it off later.

As long as you have a bankruptcy on your credit reports, "instant credit" should not be in your vocabulary. Take the time to fill out your applications strategically.

Do not be pressured into filling the application out on the spot to get instant savings or whatever else they may offer you. Ask yourself if what you just went through in bankruptcy court is really worth the "instant savings."

One of the most important pieces of information in your credit folder is the summary of any credit established since you filed bankruptcy. This will become an important sales tool for you to use when you are applying for more credit. At first, there will not be much on your summary, but over time it will grow.

Here is the information you should keep in your folder about every credit account or insurance account you establish:

- Name of the lender or insurance company

- Address of the lender or insurance company

- Customer service telephone number

- Account numbers

- Type of account

- Date opened

- Original balance

- Monthly payment — if it is an installment account

- Credit limit — if it is a credit card account

When you open an account, keep the contract documents in a safe place, in a separate folder from your credit folder. You will want to keep the contract or lending agreement, your monthly statements or bills, and any written communications you receive from the lender or insurance company.

COMPLETE EVERY QUESTION ON A CREDIT APPLICATION — EXCEPT ONE

If you leave blanks on a credit application, lenders may think you are trying to hide something and classify you as high risk. If a particular question really does not apply to you, just write N/A for "not applicable." This way you can indicate that you have read and answered the question rather than avoided it. It is always better to answer a question rather than leave it blank. Of course, it is important to answer the truth and be as accurate as possible. Also, write clearly, especially if you are writing figures such as your Social Security number or your salary. If lenders cannot figure out what you have written, they may dismiss your application. Worse, they may think you have written something you did not intend. Write slowly, evenly, and clearly.

Having a bankruptcy on your credit reports means you need to work harder to show people you are going to do everything possible to make it easy for them to work with you.

Now that you understand how important it is to write clearly and answer every question on the application form, you should leave one question blank. That is the one that asks, "Have you ever filed bankruptcy?" Do not lie or put "no"; simply do not check the box or fill in the "yes."

The reason you need to leave this blank is that the clerk who is reading your form will go ahead and put all your answers into a computer. If you fill in "yes" for the bankruptcy question, there is a high probability you will automatically trigger a rejection by the computer. If the question is not asked, do not volunteer any information. If you are working with a lender, such as a car salesman or a mortgage broker, you can tell them of the bankruptcy in person, but only if you know that it is going to appear on the credit report they review. If it is not going to appear, or if they do not use a credit report, there is no need to tell them.

If they do not question you about it, there is no reason for you to tell them.

However, if they ask you why you did not check the box, you must tell them that you have filed bankruptcy. Honesty is always going to place you in a better position. You might then have the opportunity to explain your situation rather than having a computer automatically turn you down based on a trigger response in the program.

As a rule of thumb, when applying for credit after bankruptcy, always be honest, but never give out information — especially negative information — unless it is asked for.

RED FLAGS FOR LENDERS

It is a good idea to be aware of what causes red flags for lenders in your credit application. Red flags alert the lender to the fact that there may be a problem with your credit history and that may position you as a credit risk. Here are some of the things that raise the red flag:

- A previous bankruptcy

- Multiple bankruptcies

- An open Chapter 13

- Tax liens that are settled, released, or not released

- Outstanding collection accounts

- Credit-counseling narratives

- A high debt-to-income ratio

- A post office box as mailing address

- Frequent changes in employment

- Being self-employed without two years of verifiable income

- Being unable to verify your phone number in directory assistance

- Employment as an unskilled laborer in an industry in which there is local instability

- Excessive number of revolving credit cards if you have a modest income

- Employers with unverifiable telephone numbers

- No checking account

- No savings account

- No newly established credit

If you are self-employed, there are even more red flags, but if you know what they are you can plan around them. As you enter your postbankruptcy era and begin to establish your financial basis once again, you can work your way down the list to eliminate as many red flags as possible.

Getting a Secured Credit Card

Some things are just hard to do without a credit card, from shopping on the Internet to making a plane reservation to renting a car. However, once you file for bankruptcy, chances are you surrendered all your credit cards and now it is just plain hard to get some things done, and you probably do not qualify right now for a regular credit card.

A secured card is a convenient and low-risk way for you to re-establish your credit worthiness. You apply for them much as you do a credit card, and have to be approved. There is usually an annual fee associated with owning the card. Then you put money down as collateral into the credit card account.

Most people start out by putting about $500 cash into the account. Then you can charge up to $500. Some banks will let you start out with less than $500. You can add more money to the account at any time. If you use the card wisely, the bank will sometimes increase your credit line without requiring you to add more money. If this happens, you are on your way to restoring your credit score.

Some banks and credit unions offer secured cards, so if you have a preferred bank or credit union you could start there. Otherwise, you can just call around to banks and credit unions in your area and find out who offers them and what sort of conditions they offer them under. If you are a credit union member, you may be able to get a lower rate at a credit union than at a bank. Some credit unions also waive their annual fees for members.

Not all banks offer secured credit cards, so you will have to shop around. When you are comparing terms, look at the fee structure as well as the interest rate. Ask about hidden charges and additional charges that can kick in unexpectedly. Also ask if the bank lets you charge an amount above the amount of collateral that you have paid. Some banks allow this and some do not. In addition, some will charge you high insurance fees to own the card. You want to stay away from companies that try to charge you monthly insurance fees. This is not a reasonable charge after you have already come up with collateral.

In addition to a minimum deposit, secured credit cards can have a maximum deposit, so be sure and ask about this too. What you are looking for is the highest possible maximum deposit. If you deposit an amount at or close to the maximum, and then never use it, it will help to rebuild your credit score.

Another question to ask when you are shopping around is when they convert your secured credit card to a regular credit card. Usually after two years of on-time payments it is possible to get the card converted.

There is something of a trend away from secured credit, unless you are brand new to credit. If you are divorced or bankrupt, some banks prefer to offer you a regular credit card at a high rate of interest with a very low limit to get back into the credit card game.

Your Fico® Score

You hear the word all the time, on commercials and on every credit Web site you have visited, but what does FICO® mean? FICO is a mathematical model that is used to help lenders determine how much of a credit risk you are. FICO stands for Fair Isaac Company, the company that created the original scoring model. FICO uses a formula based on many different pieces of information, including numerous addresses, alias names, occupation, length of time you have had credit, and other factors drawn from your credit history. This means that people who have never had a financial problem but are new to using credit may start out with a fairly low score.

FICO scores range from 300 to 850, where low is considered high risk and high is considered low risk. Those with higher scores often qualify for lower interest rates as well. All three primary credit-reporting agencies assign you a FICO score, but it may not necessarily end up being the same at every agency, so you need to find out what your rating is at all three.

How Lenders Evaluate Your Credit Application

How lenders evaluate your credit worthiness can differ from organization to organization. Some lenders take the information from your application and put it through their own proprietary scoring system. They will then use the score they come up with as a basis for accepting or denying your credit application. No matter what scoring system they use, most lenders evaluate the same criteria. This can include how many years you have been with your employer, the number of years you have worked in your industry, your income, your FICO credit scores, how long you have lived at your address, whether you have checking and savings accounts, whether you have had any bounced checks, previous credit history with this lender, credit references, previous credit history with this lender, amount of money you owe, debt-to-income ratio, whether you own or rent your home, and whether the telephone bill is in your name or someone else's.

The majority of lenders and insurance companies use a FICO credit score as a major part of their approval decision, so you do not need to be too concerned about an application score. You should make your application as strong as possible. Knowing what they look for and what causes a red flag will arm you in your quest for new credit.

A common occurrence following bankruptcy is that you will qualify for a house or a car but will still have difficulty obtaining a credit card. You may find that, despite repeatedly trying to obtain an unsecured credit card, you keep being turned down.

Strange as it may sound, it is true that qualifying for a mortgage is sometimes easier than qualifying for a credit card. This is especially true if you have recently filed for bankruptcy or if you have low FICO credit scores. Here is why: If you miss your mortgage payments or your car payments, the bank can repossess your home or your SUV because the items themselves are security against the loan. However, credit cards offer unsecured debt, so items purchased with your credit card cannot be repossessed. Unsecured debt is a much bigger risk for lenders. The truth is, if you have filed for bankruptcy, your FICO credit scores will generally be too low to qualify for a credit card until you have taken the time and the effort to rebuild your credit score.

As you apply for credit cards, keep in mind that each time you are denied credit — which is bad for your morale — you are also hurting your credit score. Each time you give a lender permission to review your credit, which you do on the application, a credit inquiry will appear on your credit report. Credit inquiries with denied credit lower your score. Having said that, each lender creates a set of credit guidelines for approval of unsecured credit, and they are required to stick to those guidelines unless they are a private bank. Calling a lender to find out their criteria before you submit an application could help you determine whether you even wish to apply for credit with that organization.

Even though guidelines vary between lenders, most

lenders require a minimum FICO credit score of 680 before they will approve your credit application for an unsecured credit card. If you want to give yourself a better chance, do not apply for credit until your credit score reaches at least 700.

The 680 and 700 scores apply to basic credit cards. To qualify for a better card, like a gold, platinum, or titanium with increased levels of features and rewards, you may need to attain higher FICO credit scores and higher income before you are approved. But even a score higher than 700 does not guarantee you will be approved for a card. Some lenders will not approve you for as long as the bankruptcy appears on your credit report. It is even possible to have a credit score of more than 750 and make a six-figure salary, as well as owning your own home, and some banks will still deny credit if you have a bankruptcy on your report.

Other banks may check to see if a required amount of time has elapsed since your discharge. Some have a waiting period of 12 months and others can have waiting periods that range from two to four years.

This is why it is important to call a potential lender before you apply for a credit card and find out what their requirements are for approving credit cards. If you cannot find the answers you are looking for, do not risk lowering your score by applying for credit and being turned down.

The first question to ask is which credit-reporting agency your lender uses. Do not assume that the credit-reporting agency that has you evaluated at the highest FICO score is going to be the one they use. Lenders can choose any credit-reporting agency to get your credit report. For example, let us say Equifax gives you a rating of 791 and that prompts you to go apply for a credit card. The lender may use Experian. At Experian your credit score may only be 610. Each credit-reporting agency evaluates your score according to its own formulas, so it pays to know what all three of your credit scores are. They need to be at least 680 (700 is better) at all three reporting agencies.

If your scores are not as high as you think they should be, you need to look at your negative reason codes and try to identify the reason you have not achieved a higher rating. Then you must fix whatever it is.

The first step in your credit recovery plan is to know your FICO scores by obtaining credit reports from all three credit-reporting agencies. Remember that you should always use the central government authorized Web site to get your scores at **http://www.annualcreditreport.com**.

WHAT AGENCY DO LENDERS USE?

It used to be easy to find out what credit-reporting agency your lender was using. Lenders on the East Coast favored Equifax, Experian was primarily used on the West Coast, and the middle of the country used Trans Union. That is not the case anymore. Lenders tend to choose their credit-reporting agency based on other factors, such as cost. Even though all three credit-reporting agencies used a FICO scoring model, they do not all use the same formulas to arrive at the score, so the scores can be different. Visa and MasterCard do not necessarily use FICO to determine your credit score and arrive at a lending decision, but a modified FICO formula. It is similar in concept to how auto lenders determine your credit score; they do not use FICO either.

However, all credit card lenders are primarily interested in how you have managed your previous and existing revolving credit. Some credit card companies are now using a newer mathematical model, called the FICO Bankcard Industry Option Score, in which more emphasis is placed on the statistics drawn from how you use your credit card.

If you have a history of handling your revolving credit well, your FICO Bankcard Industry Option Scores will probably be higher than your regular FICO scores. If you have managed your revolving credit poorly, your bankcard FICO scores will probably be lower than your regular FICO scores.

Since you do not have access to your FICO Bankcard Industry Option Score, the best thing you can do is continue to check your credit score in the usual way.

How Many Credit Cards Should I Have?

It would be nice if there were a universal answer for everyone's situations. "Yes, Mr. Smith, you should have one credit card, one auto loan, and one mortgage." However, that does not make sense, because every situation is different. Therefore, the correct answer is different for each of us, and it can be determined by looking at the unique combination of your negative reason codes. If, for example, one of the reason codes given is that you have too many revolving credit cards, you should close some.

After filing for bankruptcy, many people think they should live on a cash-only basis. Certainly, the popularity of the debit card has made it easier to do without credit cards, and it is a wise principle not to buy things you cannot afford. However, it is not always practical to live entirely without a credit card. In addition, avoiding the use of a credit card altogether will keep your credit score low.

HOW TO GET A HIGHER CREDIT LIMIT AND LOWER INTEREST RATE

You have broken through the application barrier and successfully been given a credit card, have used it successfully — and paid off your balance — for a few months, and now you wish to raise your credit limit. There are three factors that are used to determine your limit: income, payment history, and FICO credit score.

For example, you will not get a high credit limit if you have a low income or if your FICO score is below 600. The best way to get a higher limit is to ask your lender what their guidelines are.

Last, do not think that the higher your credit limit, the better your FICO will be. That is not so. Your score is calculated on factors that include how well you have managed your credit card over the period of time you own it and not just what the limit is. If you use your credit card responsibly, most lenders will automatically increase your credit limit over time.

A high credit limit and a low balance together are good for your credit, but as your credit limit gets higher the last thing you want to do is extend your card to its limit, even if you are in a position to pay it off every month.

IF YOU CANCEL CREDIT CARDS

If you have decided that you do not wish to keep all your credit cards and you decide to cancel them, you need to know that canceling the credit cards you have held for a long time can actually damage your credit. Part of your FICO score includes a factor known as "time in file." Simply, this means that credit-reporting agencies do consider the amount of time you have held a credit card and holding it for a long period, with a good payment history, translates into a good FICO score. They also look at the average age of the accounts on your credit report. Therefore, it is in your favor if you have several accounts that have been in good standing for a long time.

SCORING 800

There are not many people who ever achieve a credit score over 800 (remember that the highest possible score is 850). In fact, only about 5 or 6 percent of people nationwide enjoy a score in the 800 range. The rest of the population — about 94 percent or so — has a lower score, which means that almost everyone has some negative blip on their credit report. There are so many factors to think about when it comes to this 800 score. You could pay all your bills on time and not have an 800; you have to take into account that the credit company factors in things such as balance in relations to credit limit, how new your accounts are, your highest level of credit, and inquiries. So do not get hung up on 800; anything over 720 will get you good rates.

One thing that all those with a perfect score have in common is that they hold accounts that are very old, sometimes decades old. One example is a man from Georgia who has held his Sears card since 1945.

It actually says that on his credit report — opened in 1945. His lowest FICO score is 809. If you have old accounts around in good standing, it is a good idea to keep them.

Another habit of people with high credit scores is to keep credit card utilization low. Consider the following: Let us say you have ten credit cards, each with a limit of $1,000. Your total credit limit is therefore $10,000. Now, let us suppose that you have maxed out five of the ten cards, so your total credit balance is $5,000, which is half of your total credit limit. That means that your utilization percentage is 50 percent. The higher your utilization percentage, the lower your credit scores will be. Less is more, in this case. The lower the balance on your credit cards, and the less you use them, the lower your utilization percentage will be — and that translates to a higher FICO score.

Now, let us suppose that you have not used the other five of your credit cards in some time, for several years maybe. In fact, you are not even sure why you still have them. So you decide to close all five accounts. If you close the five unused accounts and continue to carry maximum balances on your other five cards, you are now at 100 percent utilization percentage on your credit cards. That means you have maxed out your credit, and that does not look good on your credit report.

So what can you do if this is already the case and you have already closed old credit card accounts that you no longer use? The first thing you need to do is reduce the balance on any remaining credit cards. Next, you could try to increase the credit limits on your open accounts. Increasing the credit limit will reduce your utilization percentage figure, but be cautious. If you raise your credit limit, do not be tempted to raise your credit card usage, or you will be back to square one.

If you are a small business, you can open corporate credit cards and use them instead of personal credit cards. That will allow you to carry a credit balance without it affecting your personal credit score.

Another thing to be aware of is this: If you call your credit card company and ask them to raise your credit limit, for them to make that determination they will do a credit inquiry on you, which can cost you negative 12 points on your credit score.

There is another type of credit inquiry known as an "account management review." This type of inquiry does not lower your credit score. This inquiry allows a credit card company to review your credit reports once a year to determine if your credit limits should be increased. If you qualify, the increase can be automatic.

If high utilization is a problem on your credit report, you will be able to tell from the negative reason codes listed in your report. So now you know how to tell if this is a problem for you, and you have some information to help you decide on the best plan of action.

There is one more effect of closing credit card accounts: The closed account will stay on your credit report for seven years, and so for that period, even though the account is closed, it can reflect positively on your overall credit history. After the seven years has elapsed, it will be erased from your credit history, and it can no longer serve you. The seven-year rule can be a good thing for you if you have bad credit history that you need to get rid of, but when you have good history it can work against you. Only information that actually appears on your credit report can influence your credit score.

In summary, if you want good FICO scores, make sure you have many old accounts on your credit reports. Do not limit your own scores by closing old accounts. You do not have to carry a balance on a credit card or even use it just because you choose to keep the account open.

SECURED VERSUS UNSECURED CREDIT CARDS

After a bankruptcy, one question many people have is whether to apply for a secured or an unsecured credit card. Remember that a secured credit card is one where you put down money in advance as collateral against the card. It works like this: You deposit $500 in a special savings account and then have a $500 credit limit. If you default, the credit card issuer simply takes the money in your special savings account.

An unsecured card is the usual kind of credit card; you fill out a credit application and, based on your credit report, you are approved for a certain credit limit. You then charge items to the card and the credit card company sends you a bill for the amount you have charged (effectively borrowed).

Which one you should choose depends on your credit history. If you apply for a secured credit card following a bankruptcy, you have a higher chance of being approved than if you apply for an unsecured card. But be careful. Not all secured cards are created equal. To make matters worse, there are plenty of unreputable organizations around, pushing secured credit cards.

To find the best credit card deal, write down a list of criteria that the secured credit card needs to meet and then shop for the best deal. For example, you want the lowest interest possible. Interest rates on credit cards vary widely, from the single digits to well into the 20 percent range and above. Even if you plan to pay off your balance in full each month, it is still a good idea to plan for adversity by shopping for the lowest interest rate possible.

Another good selection criterion is the application fee. Preferably, it should not cost you anything in fees to own your credit card. After all, the bank makes money whenever you carry a balance, so look for one that has no annual fee associated with it.

Another thing to look for is a lender who reports your payment history to all three credit-reporting agencies.

By the way, do not apply for more than one credit card at any one time. Just apply for one, use it wisely over a period of time, and be patient while enough time passes for your credit score to start creeping back up.

It is easy to be confused about secured and unsecured credit cards. You cannot tell by looking at them which is which. They both carry the logo of the issuing bank, and they can be used interchangeably with other credit cards. That means anyone who accepts regular credit cards will accept secured credit cards. But behind the scenes the secured credit card offers both you and the lender a little added protection.

BUYING A CAR AFTER BANKRUPTCY

If you did not own your car at the time of your bankruptcy there is a chance that you had to use it in the bankruptcy. Obviously, in today's time you need a car to get around unless you live in downtown New York or Boston.

Successfully paying on a car loan is another way to rebuild your credit. Once your bankruptcy closes, you can apply for a car loan the next day. In this section we will review some tips for getting the best rates on your car loan.

You should already be familiar with the first step; you guessed it — obtain a copy of your credit report. Make sure all your accounts are in order. You may see open accounts that should be closed, for example. Double-check everything in the report for accuracy.

Decide whether you need to add a statement to your report explaining any of the items in your report. If there were any truly extenuating circumstances that led to your bankruptcy, lenders may approve you for a better rate than if you were just financially reckless.

Plan Your Car Purchase

Do some work up front to determine what you can comfortably afford for a monthly payment. This will help you when it comes time to choose a financing package. Monthly payments are based on the loan amount, number of payments (over how many years), and the interest rate.

Use a Car Loan Lender

Car loan lenders make their money by finding you a loan. Car loan lenders work with several financing partners to back loans with all types of credit risk, including bankruptcies. Online car loan lenders deal with thousands of loans and can usually find you a better deal than your car dealership. Online car loan lenders will send you a check for the car purchase amount once your loan is approved, and you will use the check to pay the car dealership.

Explain Your Situation

When you fill out your car loan application, you will be asked if you have ever declared bankruptcy. You will also be asked to explain why. This is your opportunity to explain what led to the bankruptcy and what steps you have taken to resolve your financial situation. You can use this opportunity to explain any improvements that have occurred in your financial situation, and what steps you have taken to improve your credit score.

Consider Refinancing

Once you are approved for a car loan, keep your eye on future refinancing. By making regular payments on all your bills, within a year you could qualify for significantly lower interest rates. In three years, you can build your credit score to near excellent and qualify for even lower rates.

Your FICO® Auto Industry Option Score

The first thing you are going to do from now on when thinking about a loan of any kind is to take a look at your credit score, right? Well, you need to know one more thing about credit scores. The auto industry does not use the same FICO scoring system as everybody else. They use a system designed especially for the auto industry, known as FICO Auto Industry Options Scores.

The good news is that the FICO Auto Industry Option Scores are often higher than your regular FICO scores. The bad news is that you cannot obtain your report in the same way you can with your regular FICO credit score report. However, they are similar enough that, if you know your regular credit score, you will be well armed in your quest for an auto loan. Let your auto dealer know that you know your credit report score. It puts you in charge and lets the dealer know that you are doing your homework and are not going to allow yourself to be taken advantage of, but be aware that auto lenders are a little different from most other lenders.

If, on the other hand, for some reason your regular FICO

scores are higher than the scores the dealer reviews, it may be possible for them to offer you a better deal using your regular score.

Differences Between FICO Scores and Auto Industry Option Scores

The real difference between these two types of scores is that the Auto Industry Option Score pays a lot more attention to how you have handled auto credit in the past.

When car dealers look at your Auto Industry Option Score they will be interested in the way you have handled car payments in the past, rather than payments on other types of loans. For example, they want to know if you have made any late payments or missed payments altogether on your car loan or lease. They will also want to know if you have ever had to turn in a leased vehicle before the lease was up because you could no longer make payments.

Your Auto Industry Option Score will also be affected if you have ever had a vehicle repossessed or sent to collections for missed payments. If your car loan or lease was included in your bankruptcy, this will also affect your score.

Any of the above actions will affect your Auto Industry Option Score more than they will affect your traditional FICO credit score. However, if you were able to keep up your car payments when you filed bankruptcy and have not defaulted on any payments, you may end up being in much better shape on this score than on your regular FICO score. If your car loan has ever been sent to collections, if you defaulted on payments, or if you had to turn the car in to get out of the payments, your Auto Industry Option Score may not be very high. You will be perceived as a greater credit risk and you may experience difficulty trying to find a good loan package. If your credit history represents you as high risk to the car dealer, you are more likely to be offered a much higher interest rate.

Many people who are recovering from bankruptcy cannot believe that their FICO Auto Industry Option Score is as high as it is. The fact is, if you included all your credit card debt and your mortgage in your bankruptcy, but you were able to keep up car payments, things might not be that bad from the car dealer's perspective. The good thing about the different scoring system used by auto dealers is that it only focuses on what matters to them and does not include your entire financial picture.

Do Your Research

Once you have filed bankruptcy, car dealers know how anxious you are to begin rebuilding your credit, and they are going to send you to the "Special Financing Department," which means you are going to be offered higher-than-average interest rates for your loan. Here are some facts about car buying with respect to financing a loan:

Financing a new car is easier than financing a used car. New cars have incentives and/or rebates which can lower or eliminate the cash down payment needed to buy a new car. You can use the rebate as the down payment, so if you do not have a down payment, consider shopping for the highest rebate.

If you have had a car repossessed, there will be a hit to your FICO credit score. This is true even if you voluntarily turned the car back in — repossession and voluntary repossession are equal in the FICO score formula. So if this is the case with you, you will need to re-establish your credit with a finance company first, before you go to a car lender.

If you shop for your loan and look for just the right dealership, it is possible to get a new car loan at 0 percent interest with no money down. Each lender makes unique rules about credit terms and how they approve people for credit. These rules are called their "credit guidelines." You will need to ask many dealers what their credit guidelines are. Once you know their guidelines, you can decide whether you wish to apply to this dealership for an auto loan. You can ask them outright if they offer auto loans to people with a bankruptcy, and if so, what their terms are under those circumstances.

At some point you will have to discuss the bankruptcy with the dealer you intend to work with or to discover which dealer is going to the best one to work with. You do not have to disclose it right up front, but once you are coming close to a decision, it could be the deciding factor, so it is best to come clean and let them know. Some lenders will only lease to people with a bankruptcy. Others will only offer financing if you intend to purchase the vehicle. Some will use a combination. Ask the finance director at the dealership to direct you as to what structure the manufacturer prefers. Only disclose your bankruptcy if it still appears on your credit report. If it is no longer on your report, as far as the car dealer needs to be concerned, it never happened.

There is no reason to put several thousand dollars down to buy or lease a new car. The most cash you should need as a down payment after bankruptcy is between $500 and $1,000, if that much. If you need to put more than that down you have not done your homework.

A good place to gather information for great car pricing is **http://www.edmunds.com**. This Web site lists all the used car pricing and certified rate programs, as well as rates and rebates deals from every car manufacturer. There are plenty of car dealers out there looking for your business, so the more research you do up front, the more likely you are to find a great deal.

Car dealers can be very different from each other. Just because one turns you down does not mean you will not find one willing to approve your car loan at a reasonable interest rate.

If you have filed a Chapter 7 bankruptcy, is it not a good idea to try to finance a car before your bankruptcy has been discharged. It is better to wait until you have your discharge letter from the court in your hand.

If you have filed Chapter 13, you need approval from your bankruptcy trustee before you can finance another car. Research your deal and bring all the information with you to your trustee. You need to have a good reason for your trustee to approve a new loan. For example, perhaps your family situation has changed and you need a bigger vehicle, or maybe your current car is getting old, needs a lot of work, and just will not run anymore.

The worst place to look for new or used car financing after bankruptcy is your bank. The bank has no incentive whatsoever to take a risk on financing you to buy a car. The car manufacturer, on the other hand, is motivated to sell cars, so it has a much higher motivation factor to make you a financing deal. In addition, car manufacturers usually report to all three credit-reporting agencies, which will be good for your credit rating as long as you make regular, timely payments.

While you are doing your research with car dealerships and looking for the best deal, interview as many car dealers as you can. Avoid allowing them to look at your credit report until you are ready to buy. Remember, you want to avoid any unnecessary credit inquiries that can lower your FICO credit score.

If you are in a hurry, think about a "subprime" lender. Subprime lenders will charge you higher interest rates than a mainstream lender, so we do not recommend them in general. However, they are more likely to approve your loan. Under normal circumstances you should stay away from subprime lenders, but if you are really in a hurry for a loan and do not have time to do a lot of research, it could make sense for a person to consider using one. A subprime lender may be able to offer you financing if you still do not qualify for financing from a mainstream lender. This could be the case if, for example, you had a car repossessed prior to the bankruptcy or as a part of it. As with other lenders, it pays to shop for more than one before settling on a deal. There are good and bad ones as with everything else. The good ones have a tendency to stand out from the rest.

All credit inquiries for autos count as only one inquiry if they are made within 14 days. For this reason, you want to try to get several car dealers to review your personal credit reports during a two-week period. After you have done your research and selected a short list of dealers to work with, try and get them to agree to obtain the report within this time period.

If you have learned anything after going bankrupt, you will not be in a hurry to get yourself into your dream car. Start small and work your way back up. After you build yourself a good, solid financial foundation, there is no reason you cannot accomplish your dreams in time.

As a rule of thumb, a good interest rate on a new car will range from 0 to 12.9 percent. Credit unions normally have the best rates. The FICO Web site, **http://www.myFICO. com**, has a loan savings calculator you can use to figure out what sort of interest rate you qualify for on both new and used car loans based on your FICO credit score. The tool is free to use, and it will help prepare you for talking to car dealers.

It is important that you try to find a lender who will use your highest FICO score to make a lending decision. Remember, many lenders only apply for a report to one of the credit-reporting agencies, not all three. Ask the lender which reporting agency they use (Equifax, Experian, or Trans Union). There is a new credit-reporting agency called Vantage Score, but not many lenders are using it.

Let us spend a moment talking about the extras the car dealer will try to sell you with your car. This includes things like undercoating, leather sealer, and so on. You do not really need any of these things. Try to avoid any add-ons that will increase the total amount you end up financing for your car. Steel yourself before you go in to the finance manager's office to go over the paperwork and try to get them to explain all the options they are going to offer you in advance, because once they have you in the chair signing papers, you are more vulnerable.

Also, before you do the final paperwork find out what comes with the car and what is optional. You want to know that the basic price covers everything you see in the car — such as floor mats — when you make your decision to purchase it. There is nothing worse than thinking you have a good deal only to find out at the last moment, when it is harder to walk away, that the price you thought you were paying just increased.

Talk to the finance manager at the dealership first, before you see a salesperson. Find out what type of financing you are qualified to receive. This is the most important thing you can do for yourself in negotiating the best deal on a car. A car salesperson is going to try to sell you more car than you need. You know this before you even go to the car lot. So plan and prepare mentally. Do not let the salesperson bully or pester you into buying a car you do not need and cannot afford. If you talk to the finance manger first, he or she will direct the salesperson to the cars you are qualified to purchase. You do not want to get your hopes up only to have them dashed again when you do not qualify for the vehicle you have taken for a test drive.

When you are negotiating the amount of money you will need to put down on the vehicle, find out whether it includes tax, title, and license, or whether these will be figured separately. You also need to find out whether they can be included in the amount financed, if you want to do it that way. Most lenders will finance your taxes if you ask them to.

When you go to a dealer, their goal is to get you in a vehicle for a test drive. Once you fall in love with the car, then they are in the driver's seat when it comes to negotiation. You want this to be the other way around. So negotiate all the financing details before you go to the showroom to look at cars.

Do not forget that you can interview car dealers to figure out what options you have before deciding what kind of car you want to buy. When you talk to them, be careful not to give them your Social Security number or your driver's license. Once they have your identification information they can run a credit report on you, which will cause a credit inquiry — and corresponding negative score — to end up on your credit report. Let the car dealer know that you do not want them to run your credit report until you authorize it. If they ask for your driver's license "for insurance purposes" or make some other kind of excuse, you can ask them to put in writing that they will not review your credit.

Beware of the car dealer that offers you high interest and promises to refinance if you come back in 12 months. Most of them are lying to you. If you feel tempted to take them up on their offer, just call their bluff and ask them to put it in writing. Most of them will not be willing to do it. We cannot emphasize enough that the best thing for you to do is shop around and get smart about financing options.

Another important thing to remember about buying a car, new or used, is that if you do not get it in writing, it does not really count. Whatever deal the car salesman tries to sell you, make sure you get it in writing. Some dealers, for example, have a fleet of loaner cars that you can use when your car is being serviced. If they tell you they will offer you a "cheap loaner insurance policy" when you bring the car in, make sure you get that written into your contract and that it is good for as long as you own the car.

Be courteous and respectful at the car dealership. Your bankruptcy is not their fault. Nonetheless, do not let them bully you into something you know you should not be buying.

When your credit scores are low, you will probably have to pay more for auto insurance. The cost of insurance should be a factor in deciding what car you want to buy. Your insurance agent will work with you to tell you what insurance rates you will be looking at for various makes and models of cars. The age of the car is a factor, too.

So now you know that a beat-up used car at 22 percent interest from Bill and Bob's economy used car lot is not necessarily your only option after bankruptcy. If you do your homework, it is possible to buy a new car at a low interest rate with little or no money down.

INTERVIEWING AUTO DEALERS

Every inquiry into your credit score costs you points on your overall score. Suppose you know your FICO credit scores are low, you suspect that your Auto Industry Option Scores will also be low, and you want to buy a new car, but you do not want unnecessary inquiries on your credit score that might drive down your scores. You should go directly to the finance manager at the dealership you are looking into. Do not even try to deal with the salespeople. You should be able to have a conversation with the finance manager and find out everything you need to know in order to decide whether this dealer makes your short list.

Because it is so important to be well informed in order to get the best car loan, here is a summary of questions to ask car dealers to find out where you will get the best deal:

- Which credit-reporting agency do you use to make a lending decision?

- What is your minimum credit score rating requirement to get approved?

- What credit score is needed to get the best interest rate?

- Do your lenders prefer offering lease or purchase financing to someone who is recovering from bankruptcy?

- What leasing and purchasing incentives are you offering customers right now?

At this point, while you are doing your research, remain open to either leasing or purchasing. Evaluate your options and incentives. The choice may come down to the willingness of the lender to make you a good financing offer.

DEALING WITH CAR DEALERS

Car dealers do not have the best reputation for being honest brokers who act with integrity at all times. Be alert and on guard against dishonesty and tricks that are aimed at getting more money out of you and getting you to sign up for the highest possible interest rate. Car dealers will play on your sense of humiliation or vulnerability following bankruptcy. If you are careful and have done a good job with your research, you can avoid the pitfalls they will try to put in your path.

Here are some ways you can protect yourself against the tricks that car dealers will try to play on you.

USING YOUR AUTO INDUSTRY OPTION SCORES AGAINST YOU

Let us say you have a FICO credit score with one of the credit-reporting agencies of 580. With a score that low, you are not likely to qualify for a loan after bankruptcy. You are headed toward a high interest rate and, consequently, a high monthly payment.

When you are working with car dealers to negotiate a loan, you should only be dealing with the finance director, never with the car salesperson. So let us say you go to a dealership, ask to talk to the finance director, and you tell him that your FICO score is 585.

The finance director will review your FICO Auto Industry Option Score, which you cannot access, and determine that this score is higher than your FICO score. He does not tell you that, though.

Since you have a higher Auto Industry Option Score, you should qualify for a better interest rate — but only if the finance director is totally straight with you. But he stands to make more money off of you if he does not disclose this important little nuance to you.

An unscrupulous car dealer may not tell you what your Auto Industry Option Score comes out to.

"PLAYING THE SPREAD"

This is another unscrupulous trick that car dealers use to get you to pay more than you need to.

A car dealer can pull up to six scores on you; one from each of the credit-reporting agencies for your regular FICO score and one from each for your Auto Industry Option Score. Chances are that these scores are all going to have some variation. They are unlikely to be identical. Which one will the car dealer use? Well, that may depend. They may use the highest one when they quote your interest rate, but a lower one when they go to the bank for financing. This means there is a difference they can pocket themselves. To do this they will make you think you have lower scores than you might really have.

So how do you protect yourself against these scams? Knowledge is power. First, you should always know your FICO scores. Second, you should not disclose that you know these to the finance director right away. When you are in the final stages of the negotiation and you have allowed him to pull your credit report ask him what your scores are. If the number he comes up with is higher than you expect, do nothing. However, if you know that your scores are higher than he is telling you, pull out your reports and show him. There is a possibility that he will use your highest score, especially once he knows that you have done your homework and you are not ignorant. It is harder for people to take advantage of us if we show them we have knowledge about the process.

Unfortunately, it is not possible to find out our FICO Auto Industry Option Scores, only our regular FICO scores, but do the best you can with the information you can get. One additional thing you can do is ask the lender to show you their tier levels. Tiers are essentially charts lenders use that have different interest rates based on your scores. You want to see which tier you fall in. If they will not show these to you, this should be an indication of what type of person you are dealing with, but you can still try to get them to explain it to you verbally.

If you know that you are likely to have poor auto credit, because you met some of the criteria talked about above, then when you are interviewing car dealerships, be on the lookout for one that uses traditional FICO credit scores. That way you stand a better chance of getting a more reasonable interest rate. You probably will not find very many, since most dealers use the FICO Auto Industry Option Score.

MORE ABOUT AUTO LENDERS

There are three types of lenders you should consider following your bankruptcy.

The first kind, known as "captive lenders," are the car manufacturers themselves. The manufacturer is the most likely to make you a good deal because they want to sell cars.

The worst captive lenders you can use to obtain an auto loan following your bankruptcy are the luxury lenders, such as BMW, Mercedes, and Porsche. However, some of the mainstream lenders will also make it difficult for you. Among the worst of the mainstream captive lenders are Honda, Kia/Subaru (which uses Chase Automotive), and Toyota. These lenders will make it hard for you to borrow from them once they know you have filed for bankruptcy. You stand a better chance of getting financing from one of these if you are at least a few years away from your bankruptcy and they will be looking for a very high credit rating from you.

However, there may be times when they offer you a good

deal. For example, if one of them happens to be a very big dealership in your town, they may be able to offer you a deal that a smaller dealership could not.

Another thing to think about is that deals do change over time and so do credit guidelines, so it is always worth exploring all your options at any given time.

After you have done your research you can narrow down your choice to one or two auto manufacturers. Are you getting the idea that choosing the lender is the most important factor in buying a car following bankruptcy — not your choice of car?

Your second choice of lender should be a bank (but not a finance company). Most auto dealers refer to their funding sources as banks, but in fact some are credit unions and some are subprime finance companies. Subprime auto finance companies should be your last resort, because they will charge you the highest interest rate. Here is a list of subprime companies to help you avoid them:

- HSBC Automotive

- Capital One

- AmeriCredit

- WFS Financial

Your third choice of lender should be a credit union. When you research credit unions, you should be thinking about whether the credit union reports to all three credit-reporting agencies. The way to find this out is simply to ask them. Ask to speak to the branch manager and then ask them which credit-reporting agencies they use. After you get the loan, check all three of your credit reports and verify whether the loan inquiry appears on all of them.

LEASE VERSUS BUY FOR A PERSON WITH A BANKRUPTCY

If you are recently recovering from bankruptcy, the thing that matters most is being approved for a loan at a reasonable interest rate so that you will be able to purchase a car and make the car payments within your budget. Next, you want a lender that reports to all three credit-reporting agencies so that your car loan and your payment history will boost your credit scores. Finally, you need to find a lender who is bankruptcy friendly, but not trying to rip you off.

If you find a lender that meets these criteria but they only finance leases, you may conclude that leasing is a better option for you right now. If you have a choice between leasing and purchasing, it is recommended to choose the option that gives you the lower payment, because the last thing you want is to default on payments again. After your credit score rises, you can drop the lease and refinance, broaden your selection of lenders, and get yourself a better deal.

If you have a credit score high enough to meet the lender's requirement, and enough time has elapsed since your discharge to where the lender is willing to overlook the bankruptcy, then you are in a great position.

If two or more years have passed since the bankruptcy, or if the bankruptcy no longer appears on your credit report, you can choose almost any car you like. But we recommend that your research your options, as described above, so that you appear knowledgeable and in control no matter what the dealer will find out. It just makes sense to be smart when it comes to your money and to always look for the best financial deal whether you are buying a car, a house, or anything else.

Refinancing Your Car Loan

The first thing to learn about refinancing your car loan is to never take a bad deal up front because the car salesman assures you that you will be able to refinance within a year. Once a car salesman knows you are recovering from bankruptcy he will rush to offer you deals at extremely high interest rates. Then, you go back a year later to take him up on his offer of refinancing and you find out he was lying to you all along. Go through all the steps outlined above to get the best possible deal in the first place.

Let us say that, no matter how it happened, you ended up with a deal that you now think you can improve upon. Here is how you can go about refinancing your auto loan.

The first thing you need to determine is whether you qualify for refinancing or if you are better off just selling or trading in your car. So let us start with how much your car is worth.

The biggest mistake most people make when determining the true value of their car is to base their research on the private-party value. You need either the trade-in or the dealer retail value.

Several Web sites will help you determine the value of your car. A good one is **http://www.edmunds.com**. Another one is the Kelley Blue Book Web site at **http://www.kbb.com**. You might try more than one site to get a good idea of what your car is worth. When using these sites you will need to know as much about your car as possible, including what optional equipment it has. You will also be asked to estimate the condition of your car. Being fair and honest about optional equipment and your car's condition will give you a better idea of what your car is really worth.

One other thing you can try in order to find out the value of your car is to take it to a CarMax dealership, if there is one near you. They will give you a free appraisal.

Generally, there are three different values for your car: the trade-in value, the private-party value, and the dealer retail rate. If you plan to trade your car in for another vehicle at a dealership, then the trade-in value and the dealer retail rate are what you are interested in examining. Some lenders base their refinancing on the trade-in value and others on the retail value. Ideally, you want to find a lender that uses the retail value, as it is always higher.

Next, you will want to find out what the payoff amount is on your vehicle. The payoff amount is usually smaller than the sum of the remaining payments, because the monthly payment amounts include interest. If you are purchasing your car and you pay your loan off early, you will pay less in interest. To find out your loan payoff you will need to call the lender and ask them to calculate it for you.

If you are leasing the car, the payoff calculation will be different. You will need to add the total remaining payments, the residual amount, and any early termination fees to determine the payoff amount.

Now subtract the value of your car from the payoff amount. If you owe less than the car is worth, you are in great shape, and you will have more options when it comes to refinancing or trading in the car. If you owe more than the car is worth, you are not in such great shape. Owing more than the car is worth is referred to as being "upside down."

If you know for sure that you will trade in a car, one thing you can do to see if there are any extra dollars in the car is to review the insurance policy. It might be possible to cancel some of the extras like disability insurance, extended warranties, and so on. This may mean calling the dealership where you bought the car and signing cancellation forms. It may take a few weeks for the refund to be applied to your account, but it can reduce the payoff on the vehicle.

Once you have the facts about your car's worth, it is time to start calling lenders.

Credit unions and banks are the best sources for refinancing your car. Car manufacturers rarely refinance

— unless it is for a luxury car. As we have said before, make sure that the lender you use reports to all three credit-reporting agencies.

WHAT TO ASK THE LENDER

If you are thinking about refinancing your vehicle, be sure to discuss with your lender and find out what their process is for approving your refinance. A key question to ask is how they figure out the financing value of your car. Is it based on the Kelley Blue Book trade-in value or the car's retail value? Once you understand how they are figuring out the value of your car, the next question is whether they are prepared to finance you for some amount over that value.

You will also want to ask them what their credit score requirements are and which credit report they use. This will help you know ahead of time what you are up against.

On average, the amount that lenders will refinance will be about 10 percent over the trade-in or retail value. Some lenders may go as high as 25 percent above the value. So if you are upside down for more than 10 percent of the value of your car, you will need to either come up with the difference yourself or continue with your current loan until the loan is paid down to the value of the car or paid off altogether.

If you are not in a position to refinance, there is another option you can consider. It might be possible to trade in your current car for another one that offers a manufacturer's rebate. You can use the rebate to pay down the amount you owe on your current load or the amount you are upside down on. The Web sites **www.edmunds.com** or **www.kbb. com** will give you comprehensive information on all new car manufacturers' rebates and interest rates. If you can find a rebate high enough, you might be able to pay off the amount you are upside down on and still have a little left over as a down payment.

Here is one more thing to think about if you owe more on your loan than the car is worth and you still want to trade it in. Ask the car salesperson if there is any car left on the lot that they need to get rid of. Sometimes, if a car has been sitting on the lot longer than the others and they are having a hard time moving it, they might be motivated to make you a good deal. Car dealers are sometimes willing to take a loss on vehicles they are having a tough time selling because it costs more to keep these cars on the lot than it does to sell them at a discounted price.

Of course, if this happens, just be sure that the car you are buying at a discount is better than the one you already have.

CREDIT SCORE REQUIRED TO QUALIFY FOR REFINANCING

As we have said before, every lender uses its own guidelines when determining how much credit individuals qualify for, but just to give you an idea, here are some rough estimates of what kind of scores lenders are looking for:

- 680 and above to get a 125 percent loan

- 650 to 679 to get a 115 percent loan

- 620 to 649 to get a 110 percent loan

- Below 620 for a 100 percent loan

The minimum score required varies from lender to lender, and any loan over 100 percent will go toward paying off what you owe on the car you are trading in. So it really pays to use the strategies we have given you in this book to try to get your credit scores as high as possible before you try to qualify for a car loan, and it really pays for you to know what they are up front before you begin to negotiate with car dealers.

If one of your scores qualifies but the other two do not, you need to find a lender who uses the credit agency reporting the highest score. Remember that not all auto loans are approved using your regular FICO credit score. Some lenders use the Auto Industry Option Score, which you cannot access. The only way you will know for sure is to ask the auto dealer or finance organization. If they will not answer your questions, look for another lender.

If you were making regular on-time payments on your car loans at the time you filed bankruptcy, it is possible that your FICO Auto Industry Option Scores are higher than your traditional FICO scores. In that case, it could be to your benefit to look specifically for a lender that uses this scoring system for loan approval.

Even though we have said above that you can qualify for a loan for 100 percent of the car's value with a credit score of 620 or below, most lenders will want to see a minimum score of 650 from the credit-reporting agency. If your score is below 650, you are going to have your work cut out for you. In addition, some banks and credit unions may want you to wait longer than two years before they are willing to give you a loan. That is why you really must do your homework and ask lenders what their credit guidelines are for people who have been in bankruptcy.

Summary

Even though it takes seven to ten years for bankruptcy to be removed from your credit history, it does not take that many years to begin rebuilding your credit score, and you do not have to wait that long before being able to obtain loans. If you can demonstrate through your credit report that you are successfully managing credit, you should be able to get back on your feet and qualify for the best interest rates with no money down in a much shorter time. You must take action and be proactive in rebuilding your credit by learning how things are done, minimizing hits to your credit score such as loan application inquiries, and making sure you use lenders that report to all three credit-reporting agencies.

Be smart in your search for your first car loan after bankruptcy, and do not be sidetracked by the quest for your dream car. You will need to be sensible and practical and start out with the best possible financial deal and then work your way back up gradually to that dream car you have always wanted.

BUYING A HOME
AFTER BANKRUPTCY

The thought of qualifying for a mortgage after bankruptcy is sometimes one of the biggest reasons for stress following the bankruptcy itself. However, bankruptcy is no longer the permanent taboo that it used to be. There are lenders ready to work with debtors who have demonstrated their ability to build good credit after bankruptcy.

Remember that, like car loans, mortgages are secured loans, so it is generally easier to qualify for a secured loan after bankruptcy than it is for an unsecured loan. That means it is easier to buy a house than get a credit card. There are still some things you need to know in order to find yourself the best possible mortgage terms.

First, it helps if you have continued to pay on debts that were not discharged in the bankruptcy, especially if those debts were your mortgage or car loans.

Second, you will want to make sure that your overall debt-to-income ratio is relatively low by reducing credit card debt and other types of loans, especially unsecured loans. The higher your debt, the less the mortgage amount you qualify for will be.

Third, you should organize all your documentation, such as pay stubs, tax returns, bank statements, and other documentation that supports your financial picture. This step includes a thorough check of your credit reports with all three of the credit-reporting agencies to verify the accuracy of the reports and ensure that the mortgage lender is not going to run into any erroneous statements in your report. Checking your credit report before applying for any kind of loan should be second nature to you by now.

Here are some easy steps for applying for a mortgage:

- **Step one:** Never pay any money to the lender up front. The only fee you should have to pay when applying for a mortgage is the application fee that covers the price of the lender pulling your credit application. Do not pay a processing payment to process the loan. Some dishonest lenders will charge from hundreds to thousands of dollars to process the loan.

- **Step two:** Get three to four quotes on mortgages from different lenders — do not just go with the first quote. The more quotes you can get, the better you will be able to evaluate whether an offer is fair. You will want to look at closing costs, interest rate, monthly payments, and any other fees being quoted.

- **Step three:** Get closing costs in writing. Just like car dealers, mortgage brokers will spot an easy target a mile away. Once they know about your bankruptcy, or find out that your credit is bad, they will know that you are more anxious about whether you will qualify at all — and what kind of interest rate you will end up with — than what your loan is going to cost you. This means that many lenders will attempt to make their profits off you by racking up excessive closing-cost fees. Be sure you get them to explain all the fees on the quote and get closing costs in writing. Compare closing costs among lenders to see who is charging you more.

Some home loan programs require little or no time after the discharge of a bankruptcy. In addition to being the American dream, a mortgage is one of the best ways to start rebuilding your credit scores.

HOW TO PURCHASE A HOME WITH NO MONEY DOWN

If you have just been discharged from bankruptcy, chances are you have not had time to accumulate a lot of money for a down payment. No money down is the most common excuse people use to justify continuing to rent instead of becoming homeowners. Nevertheless, these days it is not hard to find a deal that will allow you to get into your own home with no money down.

The lender you need should be capable of doing a Federal Housing Administration (FHA) mortgage. The reason for this is that FHA does not use your FICO credit score to make a loan decision. To qualify for an FHA mortgage, you must meet certain conditions. The FHA provides mortgage insurance on the loans they offer so that lenders are protected in the event that the borrower defaults on payments. This allows people who have previously been turned down for a home loan to qualify. FHA loans are intended for people with low income, such as recent college graduates and newlyweds, as well as people who have gone through bankruptcy or foreclosure.

To qualify for an FHA loan it must be at least 24 months after your Chapter 7 discharge, or you should have a discharged Chapter 13 and 12 months' history of on-time Chapter 13 payments if you are still paying your trustee. It is also important to have trustee approval.

FHA loans have financial limits on them. Be sure the loan you are asking for does not exceed the loan limit for your area. Once you know what your loan limit is, simply contact an FHA mortgage lender and inquire about becoming pre-approved.

FHA LOANS

Because FHA loans are so important, we have included a whole section about them. Even if you are not considering an FHA loan, it will not hurt to become familiar with these different types of mortgages since other lenders generally offer choices along the same lines. The qualifying conditions will be different, but the payment principles will be pretty much the same.

FHA loans are among the most popular type of loan because they require very little in the way of a down payment.

To qualify for an FHA loan you must demonstrate that you meet certain criteria. You cannot qualify until your bankruptcy is at least two years old and you have maintained a good history of regular payments during that time. If your home was foreclosed upon, the foreclosure must be over three years old, and again, you must have a good credit history ever since that time.

You must be able to demonstrate that you have been employed for at least two years with the same employer and that during that time you have had a steady income or an increase in income, and the mortgage payment you wish to qualify for cannot be more than 30 percent of your monthly gross income.

You will not be approved if you have more than one late payment that is over thirty days late in the last two years.

Do you meet all the criteria listed above? If so, you should qualify for an FHA mortgage. If you do not, you now know what you need to do in order to qualify with FHA.

The absolute best way to get into a new home is to be preapproved by a mortgage lender before you even begin to shop for homes. Not all mortgage lenders are the same. You will find as much diversity in their credit approval approaches as with car dealers. It is important to find the one that is going to give you the best deal for your situation.

While prequalifying for a loan does not necessarily guarantee that you will be able to purchase the home of your dreams, it does help you and your potential lenders know what you should be aiming for in terms of house price and what you can afford in terms of a monthly payment. Prequalifying for a loan simply means that you have done the paperwork up front to determine your income and assets, as well as your debt, and you have submitted it to a lender who will look at it as if you had already chosen a house. Based on the information you give them, a lender should be able to tell you exactly what amount you qualify to receive.

The different types of mortgages offered by FHA — as well as other mortgage companies — fall into two general categories: adjustable-rate mortgages (called ARMs) and fixed-rate mortgages. ARMs are designed for low- and moderate-income families. They can work well to get you into your first home because they are designed to have very low down payment requirements and very low payments in the early years, but the payment rises over time. Fixed-rate mortgages are just that — mortgages at a fixed rate of interest over the life of the loan.

Fixed—Rate Mortgages

The most popular FHA home loan is a fixed-rate loan known as the 203(b). This loan allows individuals to finance up to 97 percent of their home, which means that you only need 3 percent of the value of the home as a down payment. Mortgage insurance is collected as part of the total monthly payment. It costs 0.5 percent of the total loan amount, which is only half the price of mortgage insurance on a conventional loan. After five years of paying your mortgage, you will have paid enough principal off on your loan to drop the mortgage insurance altogether.

There is no minimum income requirement to qualify for an FHA loan. However, your debt-to-income ratio is regulated by the state in which you live (or in which you will be purchasing a home). The guidelines for debt-to-income ratio are designed to protect you against buying a home you cannot afford.

Energy-Efficient Mortgages

This is another fixed-rate mortgage designed to help homeowners lower their monthly utility bills. If you make energy-efficient upgrades to your home, you can roll the cost of the upgrades into your mortgage. It is designed to help you make your home more energy efficient without the need to take out an additional home equity loan. Instead, you just refinance your current loan. The Joint Center for Housing Studies has determined that a substantial number of people could qualify for home loans if their utility bills dropped.

The Energy Efficient Mortgage Loan program is available to anyone who qualifies for the FHA Section 203(b) mortgage described above. The cost of adding energy-efficient features to the home must be estimated, along with the potential utility bill savings, by a qualified energy consultant. Up to $200 of the cost of obtaining the report can be included in the mortgage.

Graduated–Payment Mortgages

Graduated-payment mortgages are designed to help people with low to moderate income that have an expectation of a substantial salary increase within five to ten years. This program is referred to as a Section 245 mortgage. The mortgage will have a low principal and interest payment in the early years, but this will grow over time for up to ten years. First-time buyers who are on a good career path can benefit from this program by tailoring their monthly payments to work within their incomes as their income steadily grows.

There are five different FHA graduated-payment mortgage plans. The first three allow mortgage payments to increase at a rate of 2.5 percent, 5 percent, and 7.5 percent in the first five years of the loan. By the sixth year, payments level off and remain fixed thereafter. The other two plans allow payments to increase at a rate of 3 percent annually over ten years, with payments leveling off in the 11th year and remaining fixed thereafter.

Graduated-payment plans, like adjustable-rate mortgages described below, can be risky. If you decide on this type of loan, you have to be prepared to find the extra money, sell the home, or refinance if the payments increase beyond what you are able to pay. This plan is limited to those who intend to occupy the home they finance.

MORTGAGES FOR CONDOMINIUM UNITS

FHA condominium loans are just what they sound like — loans specifically for people who purchase housing units in a condominium building. When you buy a condominium, you jointly own the development's common areas and facilities. It is good if you are looking for a low-maintenance solution to home ownership.

Insurance for this type of housing is provided through FHA Section 2t34(c). This FHA insurance is very important for low- and moderate-income renters who wish to avoid the risk of being displaced when their apartments are converted into condominiums. The Section 234(c) program ensures a loan for 30 years to purchase a unit in a condominium building. The building must contain at least four dwelling units, and it can be comprised of detached and semidetached units, row houses, walkups, or an elevator structure.

There are some restrictions with this type of mortgage, especially those concerning whether the condominiums have been converted from rental housing. You can find out more about the restrictions from the FHA. Again, you must occupy the dwelling if you use this type of mortgage.

GROWING-EQUITY MORTGAGES

This is another loan that will start you out with small

monthly payments that grow over time. As the mortgage payments grow, the additional payment is applied toward the principal on the loan, thus reducing the mortgage term. This means that your equity in the home grows more rapidly than with a conventional loan.

There are five growing-equity mortgage plans to choose from. The first year's payments to principal and interest are based on a 30-year level payment schedule. After the first year, the monthly payments increase by between 1 and 5 percent, depending on your plan. The actual term of the mortgage will be reduced to at least 22 years — rather than 30 — and may be less depending on the interest rate you selected and the original cost of your house.

FHA Adjustable-Rate Mortgages

The FHA ARM is a Department of Housing and Urban Development (HUD) mortgage. This mortgage is intended for low- and moderate-income families who are trying to make the transition from renting to home ownership and do not have a large down payment to work with. It keeps initial interest rates low. Because the interest rate is adjustable it may increase or decrease over time. The loan is supported by FHA's mortgage insurance program. The program allows individuals who have previously been turned down to qualify for a mortgage and underwrites the mortgage to protect lenders against default so that they are more willing to make loans to low-income families.

The FHA will finance up to 97 percent of the value of your home. This is also the amount that FHA insurance will

CHAPTER 11: BUYING A HOME AFTER BANKRUPTCY   181

allow you to borrow against the home. This means that you need to find a down payment equal to 3 percent or more.

When you take out an FHA loan it might be an adjustable-rate mortgage. If that is the case, the FHA restricts the amount that your interest rate can fluctuate. It cannot go up or down more than one percentage point in a twelve-month period. Over the life of your loan, it cannot increase more than five percent above your initial rate.

FHA does not use your FICO credit score to qualify you for the loan per se, though they might look at it to determine your interest rate.

Once you are settled in your home, if the interest rate does rise, you may qualify for refinancing the home for a fixed-rate mortgage.

FHA allows for many of the closing costs involved in purchasing a home to be rolled into the mortgage so that you do not have to pay these costs up front.

The only costs you really have to pay up front when you use this type of loan are the down payments, the appraisal, title search, and any up-front costs associated with your mortgage insurance premium. Every other cost can be rolled into the mortgage.

Because FHA is a government organization, its goal is to assist and protect the public, so it has rules that limit the amount lenders can charge in making a loan. For example, FHA ensures that the loan origination fees charged by the lender do not exceed 1 percent of the amount of your mortgage.

Eligibility

Anyone who meets the above criteria for FHA loans, has sufficient cash for the down payment, and qualifies for the monthly payment on the home they choose can apply. If you choose this type of loan, you must occupy the property as your primary residence.

VA and FHA Loan Amounts

You can find out more about both of these loans by going to their Web sites. Always start by going to the proper government Web site, rather than following links to information about the loans that lead you to other companies. It is best to get the straight facts from the source. The Web sites for the VA and FHA are:

- **http://www.fha.gov**

- **http://www.homeloans.va.gov**

With a VA loan, the maximum loan amount on a purchase is $417,000. The maximum loan amount from FHA varies by state and by county.

The Nehemiah Program

The Nehemiah Program is a privately funded program that offers down payment assistance to homebuyers.

Nehemiah provides grants to first-time qualified buyers and repeat homebuyers alike. The gift funds can be used for the down payment and closing costs for FHA loan programs. It makes no difference if you are purchasing a new construction or a resale home.

The Nehemiah Program can gift up to 6 percent of a home's final sales price, depending on the seller's contribution, and since the funds are awarded as a gift, they do not have to be paid back.

To qualify for the Nehemiah Program, you must prequalify for a home loan grant through an approved lender. Once you are approved, you are referred to a real estate agent who helps you find a home that qualifies under the program's guidelines. When you are ready to close on a house — the seller has accepted your offer — the gift funds are wired to the title company and you are able to proceed with the closing.

The Nehemiah Program has many of the same requirements needed for an FHA loan. Anyone can apply for it even if you are a repeat homebuyer, and the funding or gift money that you receive from this program is yours to keep. There is no need to repay it, nor are there any income limits on who can qualify for it.

The Nehemiah Program is available in all parts of the country. If you use this program you may be able to get between 6 and 9 percent of the price of your loan to apply to the down payment and closing costs.

Buying a Production Home

New homes fall into two categories: production homes and custom homes. In a custom home, you typically choose your lot and then you choose your floor plan, fixtures, and everything that goes into the home.

With a production home, you are buying a prebuilt home. Production homebuilders usually purchase a large tract of land and then build an entire subdivision. They will finish several homes, including furnishings, landscaping, and décor, and these become model homes. You can usually choose from several predetermined floor plans, and you may be able to choose other features, like carpeting and fixtures, usually from a series of predetermined options.

If you are thinking of using FHA or the Nehemiah Program, the purchase and closing will be a lot easier if you choose a production home rather than buying a house from a private individual.

If you decide for any reason not to go with the FHA, you will probably still get the best deal from a production home builder, especially if you can find one that only has one or two homes left on the tract and is motivated to get rid of them quickly. Production homebuilders are often in a position to give you a good finance deal.

Many homebuilders will allow you to paint the interior or perform other labor to finish your home. This can be worth several thousand dollars more, which you can add to your total home-financing package deal.

BUYING A CUSTOM HOME

A production home is going to be much cheaper than a custom home, because production homebuilders tend to build many homes at once, and so they get better prices on labor and materials. They also have a stock of plans that they re-use, so your home price does not include high architect fees. These homes are often built as they are sold, but once sold they are built very quickly and efficiently.

If you decide to go with a custom home, all of the costs will go up, starting with the cost of the lot or land on which you build. Some custom homebuilders stockpile land so that they can charge premium prices.

In addition, some custom homebuilders will build a home before they have a buyer. When they do this, they use a special line of credit, usually good for 12 months. That means they have to sell the home within 12 months or convert it to a regular mortgage. Of course, they do not want to do that because they want to sell the home, not take out a permanent loan on it. If you can find a custom home that has been on the market for a while and is near the end of the 12-month period, you may be able to get a good deal. Even though this is called a custom home, you will not get to choose the floor plan and so on, so the custom features are more limited.

If you buy a home at this point, you could gain instant equity.

What you are looking out for is a deep discount on the

home. If you use an unemotional approach to finding a home "bargain," you could end up with a brand-new home that no one has ever lived in for less than its true value.

Emotionally, you might prefer to find a builder and build your own home from scratch, but that will cost a lot more. The goal right now is to get back on track financially, not deeper in a hole.

Your goal for now needs to be doing whatever makes sense to build equity in your home so that your overall net worth will increase and you will be much better off financially.

While buying a custom home is a good way to acquire the home of your dreams, it is not the best way to get a new home after a bankruptcy because the end cost is going to be very high compared to a production home. Remember that you are looking for a good financial deal, with a great mortgage value and the chance to build equity quickly.

Buying a Spec Home

Spec homes, also called builder's spec homes, are homes that may have been used as model homes, or simply homes that have been built in anticipation of early sales. Maybe they did not sell as anticipated, or in the case of a model home, the rest of the homes have been built and there is no further need for the model. While builders have these homes in their inventory, they continue to cost them money in payments, taxes, utilities, and so on. Therefore, builders are motivated to sell at good prices. If you can find a good spec home that you like, you are in a good position to negotiate with the seller.

That is where buying without emotion comes in on your part. If a buyer does not come forward, the builder will be forced to lower the price. With just the right deal, you can make money on the home the day you close on it. However, you do not want to buy just any builder's spec home. There are different types of builder's spec homes. The builder's spec homes you will make the most money on have these characteristics in common:

1. They have been built by custom homebuilders.

2. The home has not sold for a year or longer.

WHEN NOT TO BUY A HOME

Even though this chapter has made it sound easy to buy a home after bankruptcy, there are some good reasons why it might not the right thing for you at this time. For example, if your bankruptcy was too recent and you do not meet the FHA time requirement, you may just have to wait a little longer before being able to purchase a home.

Another reason why it might not be right for you now is if you live in a part of the country in which home prices are out of reach and renting may be your only option.

But it does not hurt to know your facts and make preparations so that the moment the time is right, you will be ready.

Where to Buy Your Home

When you are ready to buy your first home after bankruptcy, be aware that the mortgage vehicles described above are good ways to get into a new home. However, these methods are not designed for building equity quickly, just for being able to afford payments. You should not expect to build equity too quickly using these approaches, and you should be prepared to wait for three to five years before it will make sense for you to move or refinance without losing money. Ask your lender about an FHA Streamline that may help lower your monthly payment after 12 on-time payments if interest rates fall during that time.

If building equity is important to you, you will be much better off in an appreciating housing market. Some cities are better than others. You will need to research home markets in different parts of the country. Certainly, you will not want to buy a home in an area in which house prices are either not rising or, worse, actually falling.

Standard & Poor's Case-Shiller Home Price Indices monitor the sales price of homes in various regions around the country. Using the data they collect, they are able to report on whether house prices overall are falling or rising, and what parts of the country are experiencing higher-than-average increases or decreases in prices.

If you decide to purchase in an area of falling prices, your chances of building equity quickly — even if you find a great deal up front — are reduced. In general, you want to look for stable areas where house prices are holding steady or increasing. If house prices are doing badly overall, you should look for an area where they are not falling as fast.

If choosing the area for buying a home is not an option for you, and you see that home prices in your area are falling, then you might decide that this is not a good time to buy and you can do better by continuing to build your credit history and saving for a bigger down payment until the market turns around. You can track Case-Shiller indices on their Web site at **http://www.standardandpoors.com**.

Instant Equity

In his article "How to Buy a New Home and Make Money at Closing After Bankruptcy," bankruptcy expert Stephen Snyder explains how to base your home-buying decision on the numbers, rather than on emotion. One of the biggest traps that homebuyers fall into is falling in love with a home that they just have to buy, without working the numbers.

If you are recovering from bankruptcy, your number-one goal should be to rebuild your credit, qualify for the best deal possible, and get back on track financially. If you eliminate the emotional aspect of buying a home and focus on how much it is going to cost you, as well as how good the chances are for appreciation, then you will make a much smarter decision.

Qualifying for a Mortgage After Bankruptcy

In this section we will discuss the emotions and feelings

you may be experiencing and help you overcome the fear of trying to qualify for a mortgage. There are several reasons fear might be stopping you from trying to qualify. It might be that you think you could qualify, but you are afraid to apply because you are self-conscious about the fact that there is a bankruptcy in your past. You may also be afraid that you will not be able to tell whom you can trust. After all, the stories of people being ripped off after bankruptcy are endless, and it is true that there are many organizations out there just waiting to take advantage of your vulnerability.

These fears play on your mind and drain you of self-confidence in your own financial decision-making ability.

There are more practical issues to consider, too. How do you know how much money you will need? Can you really qualify this soon after your bankruptcy? What if you do qualify and then cannot make the payments? Are your credit scores good enough?

It is a hard decision to make, and when you are ready to make the decision to go ahead, you need to be armed with the right information and know that you stand a high chance of qualifying. As stated before, you do not want to get a credit inquiry on your record and a disqualification to go along with it. That is not going to help your credit recovery process.

So let us try to tackle some of these questions and help you make a decision as to whether you are ready to start the process of applying. Let us start by presenting some positive things that will come out of applying for and qualifying for a mortgage:

- It will help to re-establish you as a good credit risk.

- Making regular mortgage payments significantly boosts your credit rating.

- When you apply for other types of credit, having a mortgage is a bonus.

In most states, buying a home is still cheaper than renting one. You can benefit greatly from this if you can find a good loan with no money down and make an emotionally detached decision based on good financial sense.

Your mortgage interest and the property taxes are tax-deductible. Not only will you save money over renting, but your income taxes will go down as well. In the early years of a mortgage, the interest portion of your payment is most of your payment, so the tax deduction really helps. In the year you purchase your home, you may also benefit by being able to deduct certain expenses related to the purchase.

You will be building equity in your home. Equity is the difference between what you owe for your home and what it is really worth. Property generally increases in value over time, so the longer you own your home the more equity it will build.

Owning a home improves your net worth, which in turn boosts your credit rating.

If you are lucky enough to find a market in which house prices are appreciating steeply, you can make a lot of equity very fast.

You have a lot more freedom than when you are renting. You can fix your house up your own way and play your music loud if you want to.

Only you can look after your credit. No one else can do it for you. It is your responsibility to ensure that everything is in order on your credit report and to look out for your financial well-being. That means you also have to make the decision as to whether a mortgage is the right thing for you this year, or whether you need to wait a year or two.

If it is important to you, you need an expert in your court, and finding and involving the right mortgage banker is an important step. Before you are ready to look for a mortgage banker, here are some things to watch out for that might make it difficult for you to qualify for a mortgage:

1. Being Recently Self-Employed

An unfortunate side effect of becoming an entrepreneur and going from full-time employment with an employer to self-employment is that it can make it hard for you to qualify for a mortgage until you have re-established yourself in business and can prove that you have dependable income. Many lenders require you to wait two years after such a change in employment.

The same might be true if you simply change jobs. If

getting a mortgage is important to you this year, staying in the same job until after you have been approved for your mortgage could go in your favor, whereas a job change can go against you, especially if it involves a move to a different career field.

2. Divorce

If your divorce is in the past, all financial issues have been resolved, and you have credit in your own name, divorce should not be a problem. However, if you have a divorce pending, or if there are any unresolved financial issues remaining from the divorce, the lender's hands may be tied until a financial resolution is accomplished. A lender has no idea how a divorce case may turn out, and therefore it poses a huge financial risk. This is true if you are pursuing your first mortgage, refinancing a home, or looking for an equity line of credit or any other major loan.

3. Foreclosure

Just as with bankruptcy, foreclosure can be a problem, but it need not be a deal-breaker. Certainly, time needs to pass before you can be considered credit-worthy again, and you will have to take steps to build your credit score back up.

Usually one year from the foreclosure or discharge is enough, but it may depend on your lender. A credit score of about 600 is usually required. If you have that credit score, or higher, and at least a year has passed, you will probably qualify for 100 percent financing.

Finding Your Debt-to-Income Ratio

One of the criteria that lenders use in deciding whether you qualify for a mortgage is your debt-to-income ratio. Your debt-to-income ratio is a formula for figuring out how much of your income is going toward paying your debt and how much is available for other living expenses. If your debt-to-income ratio is too high — in other words, if you already have high payments relative to your income level— you will not qualify. Most lenders are looking for a figure below 50 percent and some will want to see 43 percent.

Two numbers are calculated in the formula. The first number indicates the amount of your monthly income that the lender will allow for your total home expenses. It includes the principal and interest — in other words, the loan payment — as well as the cost of mortgage insurance, home insurance, property taxes, and any other costs that you might have, such as homeowner's association fees.

The second number is the percentage of your monthly income that goes toward your debt payments, including the first number above. Your debt includes any amount that you pay toward debt on a regular basis, such as credit card payments, child support, student loans, car loans, and other loans or expenditures. When you are including your credit card payments, use the minimum monthly payment included in your statement, and if you have an American Express card of the type that requires paying off every month, you do not need to include that. You are looking for debt that is likely to last more than six months.

Example for Finding Debt-to-Income Ratio

You can easily calculate your own debt-to-income ratio. Let us use the figure of 43 percent as the qualifying percentage. Anything higher is likely to disqualify you from a loan. So as an example, let us assume your annual income is $60,000. That breaks down to $5,000 x .43 (from the 43 percent). The answer is $2,150. This means that on an income of $60,000, payments on your debts cannot exceed $2,150 per month. If they do, you will not qualify.

Not all lenders are going to use the same numbers. The formula will vary slightly from lender to lender. When you are looking for a mortgage lender, this is one of the questions you can ask. You should also ask how they calculate the percentage so that you can figure out for yourself if you are within their limits.

FEDERAL AND STATE TAX LIENS

If you owe federal or state taxes, this can be an obstacle to being approved for a mortgage. The law is becoming more lenient regarding federal and state tax liens, so you should ask your potential lender if this is something you need to worry about.

MORTGAGE SOURCES — POTENTIAL LENDERS

Now that we have motivated you to buy your own home and given you some guidelines to understand if you will be approved for a mortgage, let us explore some of the sources you can consider for a mortgage. There are several different types of mortgage lenders. The following is a list of the major types:

- Banks

- Credit unions

- Finance companies

- Mortgage companies

- Mortgage brokers

- New homebuilder mortgage companies

- Mortgage bankers

Banks

Banks will want you to be discharged from your bankruptcy for two to four years before they will qualify you for a mortgage. A bank credit reference on your credit report is very good for your credit score. Banks also tend to charge lower fees up front for a mortgage than other lenders, but they can be the hardest to qualify to receive. Before you make your mind up, do a little research into banks in your area.

However, banks tend to have differing policies on dealing with bankruptcies. Some will welcome you warmly and others will simply turn you away. If you think you want to use a conventional bank for your mortgage, you will need to find one that is willing to accept the bankruptcy appearing on your credit report.

Many banks use the Federal Home Loan Mortgage Corporation (known as Freddie Mac) to guarantee the loan. That means that, if you default on your payments, the mortgage is guaranteed and the bank still gets their money (but you may not keep the house).

Because Freddie Mac offers a loan guarantee, they are very strict in their guidelines, and it is not always easy to qualify if you have had a bankruptcy. Remember that Freddie Mac underwrites the loan, so the bank will get its money, which means if you do not make your payments, Freddie Mac stands to lose money. That is why they are so strict. In fact, Freddie Mac prefers that four years have passed since your bankruptcy, rather than two.

If the bank uses Freddie Mac to underwrite its mortgage loans, the bank will be using their guidelines, and so it makes no difference if you have been a customer at the bank for many years. If your bankruptcy still appears on your credit report, it is probably better to go somewhere else for a mortgage to stand a higher chance of qualifying.

Freddie Mac

Freddie Mac buys your mortgage from the bank. This is known as the "secondary mortgage market." The bank makes its money up front on the loan, which is then managed by a service company on behalf of Freddie Mac. The service company keeps a small amount of the money as a service fee and sends the rest of the money to Freddie Mac. Remember that Freddie Mac is a corporation — not a person. The corporation invests the money that it receives from the service company (your mortgage payment). It makes money off the investments.

Freddie Mac uses the money it makes to keep the cost of the mortgage low. This means that, if you finance through a bank, you are probably paying lower fees than elsewhere, and that is how you benefit. If you are more than four years from bankruptcy, or if the bankruptcy no longer appears on your credit report, going to a bank for your mortgage might be worth looking into.

Credit Unions

A credit union is a financial cooperative owned by its members and formed under a charter with the federal government. You must become a member of the credit union to use its services, but you can save and borrow money at reasonable rates. Credit unions are not-for-profit organizations that return surplus income to their members in the form of dividends. They were formed originally to help people who were not able to get traditional bank loans either because they did not qualify or because the high cost of borrowing money put getting a loan beyond their reach. Today, credit unions are very popular, largely because they offer top-quality service to millions of Americans at reasonable rates. Credit unions are chartered, supervised, and insured by the National Credit Union Administration (NCUA), which is a government agency.

When you become a credit union member and you open a checking or savings account, the money you and all the other members put into the credit union is pooled. Of course, you can get your money out at any time, but while it is being stored in the bank, it is used to provide home mortgage loans. This is how the credit union can often give you a better rate than a bank.

How Do You Join a Credit Union?

To join you typically must share a common bond, such as your place of employment, or residence, as specified in the credit union charter. You then enroll by submitting an application and depositing some amount (usually $5 or $10). Once you are a member, you essentially own shares in the credit union and you will receive dividends on your money— which essentially translates to interest on your account.

Drawbacks of Credit Unions

The only real snag with credit unions if you are trying to rebuild your credit after a bankruptcy is that they tend not to report to all three credit-reporting agencies. That means that, if you borrow money for a mortgage from a credit union and you are hoping for the benefit of improving your credit rating as part of the joy of owning your own home, it might not happen. Your credit score may improve at one of the credit-reporting agencies, but may not improve at all three. Since other lenders tend to obtain reports from only one agency at a time, they may not choose the one where your credit union is reporting your good payment status.

This means that, yet again, you must be sure you do your homework and ask the credit union which credit-reporting agency they report to. If you are not happy with the answer, this may not be the best place for you to get a loan. If you can find one that reports to all three credit-reporting agencies and you can get a good interest rate on a loan, then they are just as good as a bank.

Finance Companies

Finance companies are financial institutions that specialize in providing credit to consumers. Since this is their only business and their objective is to be profitable, their interest rates are very high. Anyone recovering from a bankruptcy should not be considering going to a finance company because a reference on your credit report will seriously damage your FICO scores. Finance companies typically offer rates well above banks, and they have very aggressive collection departments for those who default on their loans.

Mortgage Companies

Mortgage companies used to be simple mortgage bankers. Mortgage loans were all they dealt in, and they financed the loans themselves. These days, small mortgage companies are frequently bought out by larger mortgage companies, who then sell the loans on the secondary mortgage market. If you use a mortgage company to get a loan, you will typically close the loan with a mortgage company but then end up sending your payment to another company.

When you deal with a mortgage company, you are typically dealing with a loan officer who has to follow strict guidelines set by the company on qualifying applicants. Therefore, they may not be familiar with servicing loans for people who have gone through bankruptcy. It is more likely to be an automatic denial based on some computerized triggers set off by your bankruptcy. It can therefore be difficult to get a loan with them.

Mortgage Brokers

A mortgage broker usually deals with several lenders, but they do not process their own loans. They make money by collecting a fee from the mortgage lender who ends up with your loan. The array of mortgage products has grown so large that it is very confusing for consumers. In theory, a mortgage broker has specialized knowledge that can assist you in finding the right mortgage, and they have access to multiple lenders, so that no matter what your circumstances, they may be able to help you find the right loan.

Most states require the mortgage brokers to be licensed. States regulate lending practices and licensing, but the rules vary from state to state.

Using a mortgage broker forces lenders to compete for your business, so you are likely to get a better deal than if you go to single lender. Currently, mortgage brokers are used for between 60 and 70 percent of all mortgages.

Mortgage brokers tend to favor conventional loans, like Fannie Mae or Freddie Mac, or they deal with subprime lenders, who will charge you higher interest rates. They used to be a good alternative to regular banks, but that is not always true now. Most conventional lenders — such as banks — have their own subprime mortgage programs that are usually less expensive.

Another problem with mortgage brokers is figuring out how to tell the good ones from the bad ones. Some only care about how much money they can make off you, and some only deal with subprime lenders and try to fit everyone into a subprime mortgage — even those who qualify for better rates. Some mortgage brokers do not deal with FHA mortgages or become involved with conventional lenders.

If you end up using a mortgage broker, pay attention to the terms of your loan. Sometimes the fine print will impose a prepayment penalty if you try to refinance the loan or pay it off early. Generally speaking, if you take out a 30-year mortgage, you will want the flexibility to make extra payments against principal without any penalties, so be sure and ask about that before you sign on the dotted line.

New Homebuilder Mortgage Companies

Another type of mortgage lender is the new homebuilder mortgage company. Homebuilders can create their own mortgage company to help people buy their houses. This can be a good deal because the homebuilder can roll many incentives into the interest rate, like the down payment, allowing you to get a home for no money down. This might be a good thing for you if you are cash poor following a bankruptcy.

As with any type of mortgage, the trick is in learning to

read the fine print and understanding exactly what you are paying for. If the homebuilder is straight with you and not trying to trick you into a higher interest rate than necessary, you might find this is a good deal. However, the only way you really know is if you shop around and compare other options.

Mortgage Banker

A mortgage banker is really just like a mortgage company or bank. It is essentially a mortgage company that loans its own money. Many mortgage bankers also have the ability to broker loans.

Mortgage bankers have the ability to keep their loans and not sell them to the secondary market. Therefore, they can be more flexible in how they apply their qualifying guidelines and can be more amenable to looking at bankruptcy on a case-by-case basis, evaluating each applicant separately rather than using a computer program that automatically rejects your application based on the bankruptcy trigger.

Using a mortgage banker is a good way to go. When you are shopping for your mortgage, here are some things to look for in a good mortgage banker:

- They can do FHA/VA loans.

- They can do conventional loans.

- They work with the best subprime lenders.

- They can broker to other lenders.

- They have access to bank programs.

The are knowledgeable and experienced when it comes to qualifying applicants of all types.

Now that you know some of the different types of lenders, here are some more things to consider when you shop for your loan.

First, obtain your credit reports from all three reporting agencies and know what your FICO credit scores are.

Next, you can begin to look for several lenders in your area who fit the categories above that you think will work best for your situation.

Then you can start calling them and asking questions. Remember not to give out your Social Security number, and tell them specifically that you do not want them to pull a credit report on you. That will come later when you have narrowed down your search.

You are looking for a lender that reports to all three credit-reporting agencies, will offer you a reasonable interest rate with no prepayment penalties, and who will prequalify you for a loan.

When you talk to potential lenders, do not just ask them questions. Pay attention to the questions they ask you. When you hang up the phone after talking to the first one, make sure you know the answers to all the questions you were asked before you talk to the next one, and so on. This way, as you go down your list of potential lenders, you will be helping them identify you as a potentially good risk. After all, once you let them do a credit inquiry on you, you only want a positive result.

Make sure you know all three of your FICO credit scores in advance. If they ask you about your scores, it is acceptable to tell them, as long as you do not authorize them to run your credit report until you are ready. Mortgage lenders usually use the middle of your three scores if your scores are different. They do not use the highest or lowest. If they ask you for your score, give them the middle one. You do not have to give them all three.

If a potential lender answers "no" to many of your questions when you would have preferred "yes," strike them off your list. This is probably not going to be a good lender for you. If you sense that they are not giving you their best service, mark them off the list as well. You are looking for a lender who is going to make you a fair deal and treat you well as a customer.

You will need to tell the lender about your bankruptcy and ask them what their guidelines are for bankruptcy cases. The lender should come back with some questions right away about your bankruptcy. Expect to hear — and be prepared to answer — these three questions:

1. When was your bankruptcy discharged?

2. Was it a Chapter 7 or a Chapter 13 bankruptcy?

3. Do you know your middle FICO credit score?

After you have answered these questions, you can ask the lender if they think you can be preapproved for a mortgage. The answer might be "no." If it is, ask them what would have made it a "yes," so that you can learn from it, and then move on to the next lender. It is just like anything else. You cannot be afraid to hear "no." Just keep trying and remember you are that much closer to hearing "yes."

Finding a Good Mortgage Broker

Good mortgage brokers are hard to find, so be prepared to talk to many of them and interview them until you find someone you think you can really trust. A good mortgage broker can mean the difference between being approved for your mortgage and being turned down. It can literally save you thousands and thousands of dollars over the life of your loan. So be picky up front, and be patient with the process.

It is better to work with a large lender rather than a small mortgage broker. A large lender will have more options for you to choose from, access to more lenders, and deals that are more competitive. A small broker will be more limited. It will take them time to find a mortgage for you, and they will probably charge you more in closing fees. A small broker will have to send your loan information to multiple lenders, and each will want to pull your credit report for themselves, resulting in multiple hits to your credit report, unless by chance they happen to be within the same 14-day period.

The best mortgages available are called "A" papers. You want to try to find a lender that has access to "A" papers.

That way, if you do happen to qualify for one, it will be available to you. If you do not qualify for one, you want a mortgage broker who will be able to find the next best deal. The broker or banker you select should also be accustomed to working with bankrupt people. If they have served bankrupt customers in the past, they are more likely to have a good idea of what they are doing and be able to help you find the best mortgage vehicle.

Another thing you want to find out about is the closing costs. Every lender will have at least some up-front fees for purchasing a mortgage. The fees vary from lender to lender. Some lenders advertise "no closing costs," but there are still fees associated with closing that you will have to pay. Ask lenders how much they charge in total to close on the loan. Ask them to name every fee and every item that incurs a charge to you.

Some lenders, or loans, require very little money down. There are mortgages where you can put as little as 5 percent, 3 percent, or even no money down. You must be careful when you see deals like this, because you may not yet qualify for this type of loan if it has not been long enough since your discharge. This is certainly something you can ask potential lenders about and find out what their response is to people in your situation. You may find that, by waiting six months or so, it could make all the difference and that might be worth it to you.

STATED-INCOME MORTGAGES

The majority of homebuyers work at regular, full-time jobs and receive a steady paycheck and a W-2 form from their employer. However, some buyers do not fit into this category. Some people own their own business, make commissions off sales, or live off their investments. Some others get their income as cash or tips, and that can be hard to document. Some just do not want to give out their financial status.

Limited-documentation mortgages are available for people who fall into these categories. They are called "low-doc" and "no-doc" mortgages because they require less documentation than regular mortgages.

A "stated-income loan" is a low-doc mortgage that allows a borrower to be approved using the income the borrower states on the application form, as opposed to the income the borrower can document. With a stated-income loan, the lender agrees not to attempt to verify the income stated on the application.

When you apply for a regular, or "full-doc," loan you are required to show earnings for two years by submitting W-2s or tax returns. Self-employed borrowers usually have the most trouble meeting this requirement, so stated-income loans were created to help the self-employed overcome this problem.

Even though lenders do not check income on a stated-income loan, they do check the source of the income. Usually they require a self-employed borrower to be self-employed in the same business for two years (lenders usually require salaried employees to be in the same line of business for two years also).

In addition to being self-employed for two years, the earnings you report on your stated-income mortgage must be roughly consistent with incomes earned in the type of business or line of work being reported. If the borrower shows an income that is at the top of the range, they may have to show proof of having significant financial assets.

Borrowers pay for the flexibility and privacy of these types of mortgages because they carry higher interest rates than conventional mortgages. Lenders want you to make a substantial down payment on this type of loan and to have excellent credit.

You should expect a good mortgage broker to talk you out of this type of loan because it costs more. Before you consider one, talk to a qualified mortgage banker and give him or her all of your information, because he or she may be able to advise you about how to document what you think is undocumentable, resulting in a better (lower cost) mortgage for you.

There are two other types of loans that are considered low-doc. These are no-ratio loans and no-doc or NINA (no income/no asset). No-ratio loans are for people who may be living off investments, whose lives may be complicated by divorce or the death of a spouse, or a career change. NINA mortgages are for people who can afford to pay for privacy and have good credit. Both types of loans are generally used only by wealthy people since they are both expensive.

The purpose of these loans is not to qualify borrowers who otherwise would not qualify for a loan; rather, it is to speed up the loan process for people who do qualify but do not necessarily have documentation for various reasons related to the type of work they do and how their income is accounted for.

As an example, a man who owns ten restaurants might apply for a no-ratio loan because a conventional loan could require submitting personal and corporate tax returns and a year-to-date profit-and-loss statement for all the restaurants. It would cost him more to pay his accountant to assemble the paperwork than what he would end up paying in his increased rate.

Another example would be a retiree who sells his business for several million dollars, invests the money, and plans to live off the interest. He is not employed, will not have a W-2, and is not even in a line of work anymore. Nevertheless, he has plenty of money and is a low credit risk.

The rate for no-ratio mortgages can start at about a half-point above the rate for a conventional mortgage, and it might be up to three points higher. Excellent credit scores are usually required for low-doc mortgages.

Stated-income mortgage loans will probably work best for someone who needs a low-doc mortgage and is recovering from bankruptcy. They are available as 15- or 30-year fixed-rate mortgages. You can sometimes get a lower rate once you have more than 5 percent equity in the home.

Stated-income mortgage loans are also available as five-year ARMs and as interest-only loans. With an interest-only loan, you only pay interest and nothing against principal, so you never really pay down the amount you owe on the house. This is not a good idea for people looking to build equity in their homes, because they will never build any.

Stated-income mortgage loans are available for single families, townhouses, manufactured housing, and low-rise condominiums.

The basic thing to keep in mind with true no-doc mortgages is that the lender only has your credit profile and property to evaluate. If you can provide verification of either employment or assets, you will save some money because you have lowered the lender's risk.

Here are some general guidelines for what lenders might be looking for with a stated-income mortgage loan. These are not specific criteria. As with all the mortgage types, each lender will have particular criteria for mortgage approvals:

- A minimum middle credit score of 640

- Five credit accounts — three from alternative sources, such as utility, auto, insurance, and so on

- Bankruptcy and foreclosures must be discharged for three years, and your credit must be re-established and be in good standing

- You need to show that you have been with the same employer or in the same business for two years

- Five percent down payment of the value of the home is required, and it must be funded with your own money. It cannot be gifted money.

Preapproved Versus Prequalified

Once you have found a lender you think you can work with, start the preapproval process so you can get a preapproval letter to use in your home search.

With your preapproval letter in your hand, you are ready to shop for a home. Being preapproved is the only way to put yourself in a position of financial power. If you find the home first and fall in love with it, you will be under pressure to find a mortgage lender quickly. That means you will not have time to do proper research and will most likely end up with a bad financial deal. It really does not matter how good a deal a house appears to be on the surface. If you cannot get a good mortgage, you could end up with a big problem later on and ballooning interest payments or extremely high interest payments that will bleed you dry and do nothing for your credit rating.

The only way you can be preapproved for a loan is if you have a piece of paper in your hand from a lender who has already run a credit report on you and promised to provide a loan for a specific amount. Do not fall prey to being told you are prequalified on some vague worksheet that a loan officer or a real estate agent runs on you. Credit card companies use the same ploy. They tell you that you are prequalified based on income or such-and-such criteria, but once you apply, the real credit check begins.

The letter tells every real estate agent and home seller you talk to that a mortgage company is willing to lend you money. By having that proof in your hand, you are showing them that you are a good potential customer, and this makes them more willing to do business with you. It is an important step in the process.

When you do find the home you want to buy, if anyone else is bidding on it at the same time, you are more likely to get it if you are preapproved and the other buyer is not. Most important, since you know that your past bankruptcy has been a problem, you will not be left wondering whether you are even looking in the right price range. You will know exactly what you can afford. That is worth a lot.

Here is another thought. Let us say you find a house that the owner or homebuilder is eager to sell — remember the best deal is going to be one that has been sitting around for a while and the seller really needs to get rid of — and you offer a couple thousand less than an already-reduced asking price, but you have your preapproval letter in your hand. It is going to cost the seller money to keep the house on the market while they find another buyer and then go through the process of approving them. You can remind the seller of this, and you just might get an even better deal out of it.

FIND A GOOD REAL ESTATE AGENT

A good real estate agent can be a valuable asset. Look for one who has been in business for some time, not someone who is brand new and has not established a reputation locally. Ask your (nonbankrupt) friends whom they have used and whether they were happy with the service they received.

A good real estate agent knows the market in your area and knows a bargain when he sees one. What you need is to be able to trust his opinion.

One way to find a good agent is to start looking at homes in the area in which you wish to live. Call up the real estate agent associated with the home listing and get into a conversation with her. You can even sign up to have her show you a couple more homes. You are going to be interested in which lenders she recommends to you, how many lender recommendations she can make, and whether she listens to you. For example, let us say the agent asks you what you are looking for in a home and you say, "I need at least two full bathrooms and a large kitchen." The following weekend the agent lines up some homes for you to look at. Not one of them has a large kitchen and two of the four only have 1.5 bathrooms. Either this real estate agent is not listening to you, or the home you are describing does not exist in your price range. You need to be honest with yourself about what you can expect for your money and then you need to decide if this is the best agent to work with.

What about the location of the homes? Some real estate agents only work certain sections of the market and will focus on selling you homes in that area. If you are looking to move into a different area, that might be a reason to find another real estate agent.

By the way, you need to actually go and look at the homes. Do not decide if the agent is listening to you based on the description and photo given to you, because photos can be deceiving. After you see the type of home this real estate agent is pointing you toward, you will have a better idea of whether or not this is a good agent for you.

RENTING AN APARTMENT AFTER BANKRUPTCY

There is a certain amount of pride that goes along with owning your own home, and besides, it is usually cheaper in the end to buy rather than rent. However, timing is everything, and at this moment of your life, as you rebuild your financial affairs after bankruptcy and enter into your two-year waiting period, it just makes more sense for you to rent.

Renting gives you time to allow your FICO score to rebound, pay off any outstanding bankruptcy debts, and gather your momentum. Besides, if you are really in dire straits financially, it pays to remember that, while paying a mortgage and owning your own home is cheaper in the long run, in the short run it can cost you a lot of money in repairs, landscaping, utilities, and so forth, most of which may be covered in your rent. If you own your home, you are also expected to own a lawnmower, pay for garbage collection, keep the trees trimmed, keep the fence in good repair, and so on. If money is tight, this can make owning a home more of a liability than a joy. So renting has its place.

If you do have to rent for a while, there are ways to rent

and still make money to collect for your down payment. Consider renting a house instead of an apartment and rent out the extra rooms to make money. You can learn how to do this by reading a book called *Living With Tenants: How to Happily Share Your House with Renters for Profit and Security*, by Doreen Bierbrier.

If you do decide to rent to roommates, you should carefully screen them and be very picky about whom you decide to rent to. Remember, you will be living with them for a while.

If you live near a university or college campus, students can be a good source of renters, and they tend not to stay too long, so that can sometimes be a quick source of extra income with an easy out for you. Graduate students are best because they tend not to party as much as undergraduates do, and they are usually more serious.

You can ask renters for the first and last months' rent, as well as a security deposit up front. By doing this you safeguard yourself against them defaulting on rent payments. If they get behind, you have at least one extra month's rent in hand.

If you take in renters to use up the extra space in your rental house, you should be able to cover quite a bit of the rent and be able to put your own money aside as savings or to pay down some of your debt.

Working With Your Lender

Even though you have gone to some trouble to interview potential lenders and make the best choice possible, do not expect it to be smooth sailing from there. A good lender should be willing to help you work through hurdles, but remember, you are not coming into this with the best possible credit profile, and so there may be times you become frustrated with the whole process.

A loan that may normally take two to three weeks to process for some people may end up taking a little longer than expected in your case. This is something you just need to live through and provide the lender with as much information as possible whenever you are asked.

MORTGAGE INSURANCE

When you put down less than 20 percent of the value of your home, you are required to pay private mortgage insurance (PMI). Usually PMI is rolled into your house payment so you do not have to remember to pay it separately. After the equity in your home reaches 20 percent — because you have paid off enough principal over the course of time to own 20 percent of your home — you are entitled to eliminate the PMI, which reduces the amount of your monthly payment.

What you are getting with PMI is protection against defaulting on your mortgage. If you lose your job, become disabled, or are otherwise unable to make your home payment, the PMI is designed to help you. If you do eliminate the PMI, you might want to look into your own mortgage insurance if you feel you need insurance protection.

Underwriting the Loan

When you apply for a loan, the loan goes through several stages on its way to being approved. First, the information on your loan application has to be verified. Second, the property has to be assessed to ensure that you are not paying more for it than it is worth. Then a title search has to be conducted to ensure no one else has a lien on the property or any rights to it. After that, the loan is underwritten. This means that a trained professional reviews all the information as a complete package, verifies your credit worthiness, and finally issues a decision as to whether to approve the loan.

Increasingly, much of the analytical portion of underwriting is performed by technology through artificial intelligence and the use of databases. There are general secondary market underwriting guidelines, but many variables are considered in the analysis.

Here are some of the things the underwriter looks at:

- How much your house will cost you monthly and your total debt obligations to see if you are within your debt-to-income ratio limits.

- Total monthly income available to be used for the mortgage, including yours and your spouse's — or anyone else who may be a coapplicant on the loan. The income can be derived from any source, including interest income, alimony, and so on, but the income must be continuous income, not occasional, or likely to terminate in the near future.

Income from salary usually requires two years of steady employment.

- Commissions, bonuses, and bonus commissions can all be used as income. If you regularly receive commissions and bonuses, they will be averaged for a two-year period and the average figure is what will be used in the debt-to-income ratio calculation. They must also show up on your federal income tax return and your year-to-date earnings from your employer (pay stubs).

In the case of self-employment income, the underwriter will average the income derived through self-employment for the last two years. The figures used are those reported in your federal tax returns and the year-to-date earnings from a profit and loss statement for your business.

Other income that can be used for loan qualification may be derived from rental properties, interest, dividends, pensions, and Social Security.

Income-to-debt ratio is determined using the income of all borrowers together. Individually you may have one income-to-debt ratio and your spouse may have another, but the underwriter will combine all income and all debt to produce a single figure. Two different types of ratio are actually calculated: the Primary Housing Expense and the Total Obligations Income Ratio.

The underwriter also examines and verifies the funds you intend to use to close on the loan. He will look at the source of the funds you are using for the down payment.

In general, it is acceptable to use cash you have in a bank or an investment company. Other types of funds are also acceptable, among them stocks, bonds, and mutual funds. You may be required to submit statements for two to three months on any accounts that hold your funds.

The sale of existing property is also a valid source of funding for a down payment and closing costs. The value of the funding comes from the equity in your home. You will have to include the sales price of your existing home on your mortgage application. When you sell your home you will pay off the existing mortgage from the proceeds, along with any home equity loans that exist against the property; any remaining money is your equity in the home. This is the amount you have available to use for the down payment of another home.

Gifts of money from family members can also be used as a source of funding for a down payment or closing costs, as long as they are true gifts and do not require repayment. Some loan programs limit the amount of money that can come from gifts.

The underwriter examines your credit worthiness as part of the underwriting process by looking at your credit scores, payment history, and so on.

As part of your credit analysis, the underwriter looks for history of mortgage debt and whether your payments were made on time. A good payment history on mortgage debt is very important, especially if you are recovering from a bankruptcy. Payments received 30 days past due are reflected in your credit report as late. Lenders vary in their strictness and some may not allow any late mortgage payments, while others may allow one or two if the rest were made in a timely way and you have inserted a good explanation in your report for any late payments.

Installment and revolving credit on your report is also examined. Credit reports indicate the outstanding balance and the terms of payment for your credit cards. They look at your payment history and determine whether you regularly pay off the minimum amount or if you make larger payments. They are trying to understand your strategy for managing debt. In addition, they look to see if payments were made on time. Usually they are not concerned with minor or isolated incidents.

They look for collections, repossessions, foreclosures, and bankruptcies. If you have a bankruptcy and you have entered a plausible and reasonable explanation in your credit report and done your homework up front to maximize your chances of being approved through this lender, this should not present a problem, especially if you have an excellent record following your bankruptcy.

They might question you about how you intend to manage your finances once you are approved for the loan. Answer any questions they have honestly and sincerely, particularly with respect to the bankruptcy. Let them know you take your finances seriously, and you have done a lot of work to rebuild your credit score.

Underwriters look at the property appraisal. Even though they are not professional appraisers, they review the appraisal to verify that it meets the mortgage requirements and sometimes they ask for additional information to verify the value of the home. They may call for a second appraisal if there is any doubt. A review appraisal can be done using the original appraisal, or an appraiser may go back out to the home to perform a site inspection.

COMPENSATING FACTORS

While underwriters are evaluating your application, they do not just look at the number. They make use of compensating factors in the evaluation — things that can explain or offset defaulted or late payments. Loan applicants do not always fall into neat compartments. Many variables go into a person's overall credit history. For example, even though you have bankruptcy in your credit report, underwriters will look for positives, like your savings history, long-term employment with the same company or in the same career field, and making payments on your credit card that are regularly above the minimum. They will also look favorably on a large down payment or a cash reserve following close of escrow that means you have not stretched yourself to your financial limit.

THE APPROVAL DECISION

The underwriter comes to a decision after reviewing the entire loan package. If everything is in order and there are no issues, the underwriter can issue an approval with no conditions. However, if there are any questionable issues identified in the application, there may be some conditions to the loan approval.

"Prior to Document" Decision

The first type of condition is called "prior to document." In this case, the loan is approved but you must provide a certain document (or documents) before the money is made available. This means that the underwriter just needed a certain kind of document to back up your application, like a recent pay stub, for example, to validate your income. After you produce the missing document, the loan documentation is drawn up and the closing process is allowed to continue.

"Prior to Funding" Decision

A "prior to funding" condition is imposed if funding that you indicated you would have in the application is still pending. This will be the case if you are selling your old home in order to qualify for the loan on the new home. Technically that money is not available until you have sold the home, paid off the remaining loan, and pocketed the expected profits. After the home is sold — or whatever the condition is met — and the expected funding is available, then the closing can proceed.

A Suspended Decision

The underwriter cannot make a decision under some circumstances. Perhaps the application paperwork is incomplete or raises issues that are not resolved. The underwriter may ask for additional information from you before making a decision. Examples of issues that may cause a suspension are long periods of unemployment, or missing or nonexistent tax returns. Gaps in your history make it difficult to perform an accurate assessment of your credit worthiness, and similarly, the underwriter does not have any real negative information to use as a basis for denying the loan.

Denial of the Application

Finally, one other outcome is possible. The loan may be turned down if the loan file is substantially lacking in evidence that you are creditworthy, well funded, and likely to keep up with payments.

Before denying your application, underwriters will check to see if you meet the minimum standards for secondary market investors, and if you do they may pass your loan through to a secondary mortgage company.

If your application is not cut and dried, it may feel like you are in a never-ending paperwork nightmare. Underwriters may hold up the approval to ask you for letters of explanation for items in your credit report. After they receive those, they may hold it up again to ask you for some other document. The process can be lengthy, but a decision will be forthcoming. If you have been conscientiously building back your credit score since your bankruptcy, done your research before you applied for the loan, organized your paperwork, know your credit scores, and filled out the application as well as you could, the chances are the final decision will be positive and you will be able to move forward and close on the home.

Home Inspections

When you make the decision to buy a home, a lot of

work goes into the process of building up your credit, researching mortgage lenders, interviewing real estate agents, getting preapproved for your mortgage, and finally, at the end of a long road, the ultimate reward of owning your own home. However, before you get there, one last thing we should talk about is ensuring that the investment you are about to make is a sound one.

A good home inspection will allow you to receive in writing a detailed analysis of the condition of the home you are buying. It can provide you with leverage for negotiating the price of the home, and it will let you know whether there is a major unexpected expense around the corner — a leaky roof or dry-rot in the bathroom floor underneath the flooring.

A standard home inspection report will provide a report on the condition of the heating and air conditioning systems, interior plumbing and electrical systems, the roof and attic, basement and foundations, walls, ceilings, floors, windows and doors, and any other structural components, including the deck or patio. The report will include the age of the house, its general condition, and property outline. It is best to have the report done by a professional home inspector. You can also get additional, optional services, such as radon testing.

Do not rely on your own judgment for inspecting the property. A professional has been trained in what to look for to pinpoint structural damage or the need for maintenance. They are also impartial and looking at the home for problems with a keener eye than you are after months of preparation. Now that you finally have your eye on the prize, you may not be entirely objective in surveying the property.

Your real estate agent will be able to recommend a good home inspector. As with choosing your lender and your real estate agent, you will want to be sure that you are choosing someone reputable who will provide you an accurate assessment for a reasonable fee.

When you find the home you intend to buy, before you sign the contract, make sure there is a clause in the sales contract for a home inspection. You want your purchase to be contingent upon the findings of a professional home inspection. If the home inspection tells you that the house is not in condition, you need an out without losing your earnest money or your down payment.

What if the Report Indicates Problems?

If the home inspection report indicates problems with the home, you have some choices. You can choose to go ahead with the sale, you can try to get the seller to make the repairs, or you can cancel the contract and look for another home. If your budget is going to be tight enough that it will not accommodate the necessary repairs, and you cannot get the seller to make a price allowance or perform the repairs prior to selling, then you might have to give this house up and keep looking.

Here is a list of some of the features of your new house you want the inspection to cover:

- **Siding** — condition free of dents or buckling

- **Foundation** — no cracks or water seepage

- **Brick exterior** — no cracked bricks or mortar pulling away from bricks

- **Insulation** — condition, adequate rating for climate

- **Doors and windows** — do they open and close properly, condition of locks, weather stripping, and seals

- **Roof** — age, condition, pooling of water, loose shingles, loose gutters

- **Ceilings, walls, and moldings** — loose pieces, drywall condition, cracks

- **Porch/deck** — loose railings, steps, loose or missing boards, rot

- **Electrical wiring** — condition, fuse box, circuit breakers, number of outlets in each room

- **Plumbing** — poor water pressure, banging pipes, rust spots or corrosion, leaks

- **Water heater** — age, size for household, energy rating

- **Furnace/air conditioning** — age, energy rating

- **Garage** — condition, cracks, door mechanism

- **Basement** — water leaks, musty odors, or signs of mold

- **Attic** — adequate ventilation, water leaks from roof, insulation

- **Septic tanks (if applicable)** — adequate capacity for the percolation rate in your area

- **Driveways/sidewalks** — cracks, heaving pavement, crumbling pavement

OTHER CONSIDERATIONS WHEN YOU BUY A HOME

Owning your own home is part of the American Dream. It is one of the reasons that millions of foreigners from around the world flock to our shores. A home represents your personal security, your financial success, an investment, and a tax write-off. It is right that you should want to own a home, and you have the right to pursue the dream — even after bankruptcy.

However, you must factor maintenance in to your decision. Once you pick up the keys and move in, the real expense kicks in. Any maintenance items that were uncovered during your inspection report are going to become obvious right away and start to prey on your peace of mind.

Along with that, the general expense of running a home now begins and starts to eat at your budget quicker than you anticipated. There are water, sewer, and trash bills, property taxes, and homeowner's insurance. Plus there are the things you want to buy to make your house your home: furniture, wall hangings, a big-screen TV, and the things you need to buy just to keep the running of your house under control, such as trash cans, a vacuum cleaner, and a lawnmower. It all adds up.

Do not overestimate your income when determining your price range. The amount you qualify for is not necessarily the amount you can afford. In fact, the amount you can afford can vary quite widely from the amount you qualify to receive. Ideally, you want to run some budget numbers, determine what bills and expenses you think you will have in addition to the mortgage payment, and see if your take-home pay will cover that amount. If not, you might want to think about what house payment you can really afford, and have your bank lender reverse engineer the numbers to come up with a lower house price.

Location, Location, Location

Do not buy your house thinking that you will live there forever, especially if your choice of house is based on sensible financial logic more than an emotional selection based on "falling in love" with the house. Chances are, after a few years you will acquire equity in the home, a better salary, and improved credit, and you will want to trade up. On average, people keep their homes for five to ten years.

Your choice of home needs to factor in the resale value of the home, so that when it is time to move you will not have an anchor that will not sell on your hands, weighing down your financial capacity to qualify for a better home.

Keep these things in mind when you purchase:

- Resale value will increase faster if you are located near a growing city.

- People will pay premium prices to live in the best school district — just so long as the home is not right next to the school, a church, the local industry belt, or a big shopping plaza or mall.

- The property tax rate is lower outside the city limits.

If resale is on your mind — and it should be — remember that the buying public is conservative. Resale on a home generally goes down if you do "strange" things to the inside, such as painting one room all black, removing or rearranging walls to create an unusually-shaped living area, or performing any sort of alterations to the house that are unusual and hard to undo.

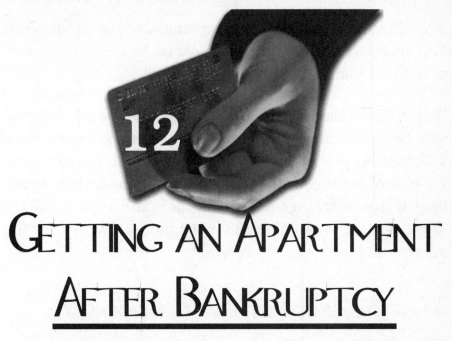

GETTING AN APARTMENT
AFTER BANKRUPTCY

If you are bankrupt and you must rent an apartment, there are some things you can do to help yourself get approved by the landlord.

First, make sure you know your FICO scores by purchasing your credit report or getting your free copy if you are entitled to one. Then, make a list of the apartments in which you are interested. You can then call each apartment complex and ask to speak to the apartment manager. Tell him you are interested in renting an apartment in his complex and you have some important questions.

Once you are speaking with the apartment manager, ask him if he has previously rented to tenants who had declared bankruptcy. If the answer is yes, you can ask what the credit guidelines are for being approved.

You will want to ask what credit-reporting agency he uses to make a rental decision. You should also ask what credit score he looks for before approving a rental agreement. You could tell him what your score is and ask how it sounds to him.

If it sounds like he is going to approve you, next you will need to know how much of a security deposit you will have to pay and what sort of income level you need to qualify for the apartment you are considering. Some apartment-rental agencies will look for your monthly gross income to be three times the monthly rental for the apartment.

WHAT THE APARTMENT MANAGER LOOKS FOR

When deciding whether to accept you for the apartment, the manager or rental agency usually considers three factors:

1. Whether you have a good rental history. Some apartment complexes will require you have at least 12 months of rental history before they rent to you.

2. Whether you have any utility collections on your credit reports.

3. Whether you have ever been evicted.

Every apartment management company has its own credit guidelines for renting to people after bankruptcy. Some will require two years after discharge. Others will want four years. Most will only require you to be discharged. However, renting apartments is a business, and you need to consider the time of year, how many vacant apartments there are in the complex, and the general attitude of the property manager. Some apartment managers will be quite flexible, while others may not.

Keep your eye out for "move-in specials." Sometimes property owners will run a special deal like one month's free rent if you move in before a certain month. If they are running a special, it is a good sign that the occupancy rates are low and that means they may be more willing to work with someone who is recovering from a bankruptcy.

Also, keep in mind that apartment complex managers are able to override a credit decision if you can show them some evidence that you will be able to make your rent payments every month — like an earnings slip or evidence of making payments on a regular basis.

Just like applying for loans, when it comes to your credit situation, it is best to be honest and up front. Tell people about your situation and ask them what their approval guidelines are. They are going to find out eventually when they run the credit check. If you have told them what to expect and you are generally behaving like a sensible person who is showing responsibility in managing your financial affairs and your credit score, you will not have too much to worry about.

In keeping with everything you have learned so far, do not let the apartment manager run your credit report. You only want one credit hit on your report after you have done your research, narrowed down your choices, and selected the apartment complex where you think you will be approved and can afford to live. You do not want multiple hits from various inquirers all over town. As you know, that does not help your credit score. Be aware that if you give out your Social Security number and sign a credit application, you are more than likely authorizing the apartment manager to run your credit report, so keep your Social Security Number to yourself and do not sign anything until you are ready for the credit check.

If the apartment manager has a problem with you not giving out your Social Security number, explain that you have recently pulled your FICO credit score and are willing to share the number with him, but you simply must reduce credit inquiries on your report because you are trying to keep the score as high as possible.

Try to stay away from using a co-signer. Do not listen to apartment managers who insist that you use a co-signer because you have been bankrupt. You do not need a co-signer. If you do not meet the credit guidelines without a co-signer, there are other ways to get around the credit guidelines, such as paying a larger deposit.

A survey of apartment complexes in Indianapolis showed that nearly 87 percent of the apartment managers were willing to work with bankrupt debtors. So do not give up the search. Be persistent and keep looking until you find an arrangement that will work for both you and the apartment manager.

Another Way to Rent

Here is another approach you can try. Find an individual landlord rather than a complex with a property owner and an apartment manager. An individual landlord may be more willing to approve you, and she does not have to work within the strict guidelines imposed by an organization.

Some people say that renting from an individual is easier and less tedious than dealing with a traditional apartment complex. If you use an individual landlord, it may be possible to avoid a credit check altogether, especially if you can show him or her your recent report. It will be less hassle for him to use a copy you already have handy, providing it is not outdated. You may also be able to avoid putting down a large security deposit.

Another advantage to renting from an individual is that you can deal more reasonably with a person than an organization. An individual landlord is going to be swayed by whether they like you and want someone like you living in their place, so you can try to establish rapport and get them to like you. If people like you, they are usually more open to being understanding of your plight.

RENT–VERSUS–BUY COMPARISON

If you look around you and do your research, you will be surprised at the many opportunities for renting and buying available to you even after bankruptcy and even if your credit is still less than perfect.

For example, you have learned above that you can qualify for a no-money-down mortgage after a bankruptcy (if your FICO credit scores are high enough). It is even possible to get the seller to pay all closing costs. This puts you into a mortgage with only your earnest money deposit. So, if you can get a no-money-down mortgage and get the seller to pick up the closing costs — and you think you will be approved — it may be cheaper for you to buy a home than rent an apartment.

If you are having trouble deciding which way to go, it might help you to do a comparison of the two different approaches of renting and buying. This will help you make a sound decision based on assessing the facts, rather than going with an emotional decision.

The comparison is like a roadmap that will show you which way to go. However, you must put it down on paper and get all the facts accounted for or you will not be able to feel confident in your decision.

Draw two lines down the middle of the paper to create three columns or use a computer spreadsheet. In one column you want to write everything relating to a mortgage, such as how much down payment, closing costs, and other up-front costs you really need. In the second column you want to write everything relating to renting, such as first and last month's rent, security deposit, and other moving-in costs. In the third column, you want to write down where you are now; in other words, what you can actually come up with up front. When you start to write things down side by side like this, you will soon start to see which way is going to make more sense for you.

Here are some examples of the information you should write down. You may be able to come up with more that are particular to your own situation:

- Monthly salary and amount you can realistically spend on rent or mortgage payments

- Down payments and up-front costs required for move-in

- Monthly rent or mortgage payment you think you can be approved for

- Credit score required for rent approval, for mortgage approval, and credit score you actually have (remember to use your middle score)

- Number of years you need following your discharge to qualify for a mortgage, to qualify for renting, and what you actually have

- Other criteria that will influence your decision, such as neighborhood conditions in the area you can afford to buy versus the area you can afford to rent

- Whether you will have additional expenses associated with home ownership (such as association dues, landscaping costs if you purchase a new home that is not landscaped, and so on)

Be realistic about costs. Home ownership is a wonderful goal, but it is not cost-free once you get past the mortgage. Ask friends how much they typically spend on running their homes and what some of the hidden costs are. When you lay out all the facts like this in such a way that makes it easy to see the comparison between buying and renting, the decision will practically make itself.

Alternatives to Buying a House

If you are ready to consider purchasing a home, but you are not quite sure if you want the expense of an actual house, you might be considering alternatives, such as a mobile home or a condominium.

Mobile Homes

First, let us look at mobile homes. If home equity is your goal, as well as a safe and comfortable place to live, mobile homes are not a good idea, even after bankruptcy. Mobile homes fall into several different categories. Actually, the term "mobile" home refers to homes built before 1976. After that time, the Department of Housing and Urban Development (HUD) put laws into effect that cover mobile— or manufactured — homes and how they are transported to the site and installed. Prior to 1976, standards were voluntary. Today, what we think of as mobile homes are mostly known as "manufactured homes." Manufactured homes are built entirely in a factory (in accordance with HUD standards) rather than at the site.

Modular homes are another kind of manufactured home built to the state, local, and regional codes of the area where the home will be installed.

You may also hear the terms "panelized home" and "precut home." These are homes where large sections, panels, windows, doors, siding, are built in a factory and then transported to the site for assembly.

Now that you know what they are, here are some facts about buying them:

- They are more difficult to finance.

- They are more expensive to insure.

- They do not appreciate in value like a "regular" house.

- Down payment requirements can be higher.

- They are difficult to sell.

You will be much better off looking for a small, single-family home or town home in the best area you can afford, and live in it for a few years. If your home is not making equity — and manufactured homes really do not appreciate as well as regular homes — you will find it hard to move up unless you really expect your salary to increase significantly in the coming years.

Condominiums

People buy condominiums because they want the joy of owning their own home without the maintenance responsibilities that come along with that, such as mowing the lawn, keeping up the landscaping, painting the exterior, and other upkeep tasks. What you need to be aware of when you buy a condominium is that you are not purchasing your own property, as is the case with a conventional home. You are actually entering into a communal ownership agreement.

When you buy a condo, your home will be an apartment within a commonly owned building. You are likely to share common walls on both sides, and may have neighbors above and a below you, just like living in an apartment.

The difference is that if you run into a problem with your neighbors you cannot just pick up the phone and call your apartment manager. You will have to work out the problem directly with your neighbor.

As a part owner in a condominium complex, you will be required to belong to the condominium association, run by your fellow residents — and yourself, if you choose to participate in the monthly meetings. Whether or not you participate in the meetings, you will be required to pay the accompanying fees. Association fees are not optional, and they are usually paid monthly, in addition to your mortgage. Some condominium associations will tap you further for sudden repairs to the communal parts of the building, such as hallways, the exterior, or the roof. If you do plan to buy a condo, which we do not recommend, you should try to find out something about how the association is run. Some of them can be quite political and tyrannical.

Condominiums are usually the first to suffer when the real estate market takes a downward turn. You simply should not expect to develop the same sort of equity in a condo as you would in a conventional home. If your condo association is not doing a good job at keeping up with the maintenance, the value of your condo may even drop. While you can support the association meetings, it is difficult for one person in the complex to influence the overall outcome of the meetings, so you may not have a lot of control over how the association money is spent.

Selling a Condo

The problems surrounding selling a condo may be reason

enough not to buy one in the first place. Your fellow condo owners may decide to rent out their condominiums, rather than live in them themselves. This means that the bulk of your condominium complex might be made up of renters rather than property owners. When it comes time to sell your share, qualifying buyers may be turned down because lenders do not like to finance condominium complexes that are made up of more than one-third renters.

Because of this, the value of your condo may drop to less than you paid for it.

The more the value of the property drops, the more owners are going to move out and try to recoup their money by renting the property, thereby creating a vicious cycle.

You just will not have this type of problem with a single-family home or even with a town home.

YOUR BANK ACCOUNT AFTER BANKRUPTCY

One of the steps on the way to rebuilding your credit history after bankruptcy is establishing your relationship with a bank; not only qualifying for a loan or getting a credit card, but just the basic checking and savings accounts. Immediately after you have filed bankruptcy, you may find that even opening a checking account is hard work.

If you filed bankruptcy and you still have a bank account that is in good standing, do not close it.

It is a good idea to wait about six months following bankruptcy before you try to open a credit account. The last thing you need is for your bankruptcy trustee to think that you have sequestered away a stash of money that you have not declared. By waiting six months, you give the dust a chance to settle.

It is important to have a checking account when you are filling out credit applications. It is even better if you also have a savings account, even if you are not able to put much into it at first. It looks better on your credit applications, and it gives you reason to tuck a little money aside each month to start to build some working capital for yourself. Having savings allows you to pay cash for things you need, avoiding the need to use a credit card.

Having bank accounts is also important if you intend to buy a house at any stage. In order to qualify for a mortgage you will be expected to produce bank statements (usually the last three months) to verify your bank balance — and you will be expected to have a bank balance! Lenders will want to see some cash in your account before you close on your mortgage. Not only do you need to show them that you have sufficient funding to cover the down payment that you are agreeing to, but also they will want to see some left over because they know you will have some extra expenses when you first move in.

CHECK–REPORTING AGENCIES

If you overdraw money at the bank, or if you bounce checks, there is a high chance your bank will report you to a check-reporting agency. Check-reporting agencies are used by banks and credit unions to verify deposit information. They keep information about account applications that have had their accounts closed by the bank for being overdrawn or otherwise mishandling their money. ChexSystems^{SM} is a consumer-reporting agency that is governed by the Fair Credit Reporting Act (FCRA). It is run by the Federal Trade Commission, so it is a government agency.

There are many similarities between credit-reporting agencies and check-reporting agencies. Once you have an entry in ChexSystems, you have to fulfill certain criteria to have the entry removed. Your entry stays in the file for five years unless the bank or credit union requests it be removed. You can order a copy of your report and register disputes just like with credit-reporting agencies, and you are entitled to one free copy every year. For more information go to **http://www.consumerdebit.com**.

If you have a dispute with an entry in your file, you can add a brief statement describing your dispute and tell ChexSystems that you would like the statement added to your file. You can get the information on how to do this at their Web site listed above.

The simplest thing for you to do, upon discovering that you have an entry in ChexSystems, is to pay it off and get a document from them stating that is has been paid. They are not under any obligation at that point to remove the entry — unless the five years have passed — but they must mark the obligation paid.

Although about 80 percent of banks use ChexSystems, some smaller banks do not use this or any other check-reporting agencies. Some of the larger banks, like Wachovia and Bank of America, are beginning to ignore ChexSystems entries that are over two years old. Other banks may be willing to work with you if you call and ask what their policy is.

There are a couple of other check reporting agencies in addition to ChexSystems. One is TeleCheck and another is Decision Power Insight, which is run by Equifax. Some of the actions that will get you listed on ChexSystems or one of the other credit-reporting agencies, depending on which one your bank uses, are:

- Any kind of fraud you have committed on a checking account

- Bouncing a check due to insufficient funds

- Going into overdraft on your account by using your ATM or debit card

- Having the bank close your account "for cause"

An easy way to show up in ChexSystems is completely accidental: when you close your account and reopen another. It is possible that someone you wrote a check to on the old account will come forward a month or so later to cash it, not knowing that your money has been moved to another bank. This is another reason to keep good records of every check you write. Then you can easily see whether there are any uncashed checks at moments like this. It also helps if you leave a small amount in the old account for a few months to make sure all old checks will clear.

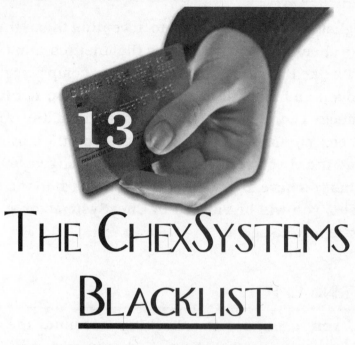

THE CHEXSYSTEMS BLACKLIST

Once you are listed in a check verification service, such as ChexSystems℠, getting off the blacklist is much like getting rid of a bad report on your credit report. Even if you pay the amount due, your report is going carry the item for about five years. Do not assume that all unpaid checks declared in your bankruptcy case will be erased, even if you file under Chapter 7. It is still your responsibility and only yours to ensure that all reports on your credit are accurate, and you need to dispute or deal with any mistakes.

You begin to figure out that you are listed in ChexSystems when you find it difficult to get your checks accepted, or if you are told by a bank that they are unable to open a checking account for you. If you suspect this might be the case, you can obtain a report from ChexSystems and find out for sure.

When stores and other merchants process your checks

through a little machine prior to accepting them, they are using a check verification system that insures your check. It works like this: the check verification company accepts the check and pays the store the amount on the face of the check. Therefore, the store is paid no matter what. If the check bounces, the bank charges you their overdraft fee, and the check verification company charges you their fee, plus you have to pay the original check amount. If this happens, you will be entered in ChexSystems or another check-reporting agency.

Ordering Checks

When you open a new checking account, the bank representative usually asks you what number you would like to start your checks. Pick a high number, such as 8500. Do not start at 1 or 1000, because this indicates to others that your bank account is brand new, sending up a red flag that you may have had to start over for some reason, or cannot be trusted yet. Usually banks will let you choose any number you wish, but if for some reason, your new bank representative will not do that for you, you can always order your checks from somewhere else. You do not have to buy the bank's checks.

You can order checks from a variety of places online. Just make sure you give them the correct bank information so that the checks will be routed properly. You may find that buying checks from one of these other organizations is considerably cheaper, especially for your initial order.

Remember to start your new checking account with as

much as you can afford. You cannot afford to overdraw a new account. With all the fees banks charge today, a minimum deposit (like $25) does not give you enough room for error. In addition, banks track when you overdraw your account, which can hurt your chances of being approved for other accounts or even loans if you need them.

GETTING A DEBIT CARD

There are two kinds of debit cards. There are debit cards that are tied directly to your checking account, sometimes known as check cards or ATM cards, and then there are prepaid credit cards that you preload with a fixed amount of money up front and you can use them for the value that you prepay. Debit cards look just like credit cards.

To use a debit card that is connected to your bank account, you need a checking account. To use a prepaid credit card you need to fill out an application and be approved in a similar way to obtaining a credit card. Debit cards are handy to give to teenagers when you want to teach them money management and give them some independence but you want to control their spending and help them not to overspend. Debit cards are also useful when you want the convenience of a credit card but you do not want to build up any more debt or end up with bills you cannot pay off.

Debit cards tied to checking accounts are replacing checks. Many young people do not ever purchase checks — they do most of their banking online and use debit cards in place of checks to access their money and make purchases.

Many banks will expect you to fill out an application and be approved for a debit card, even if it is tied to your checking account. It is a good idea to ask the bank you use what is required to be approved for a debit card. Ask them if they will do a credit inquiry. If so, ask them what the criteria is for qualifying. Remember you do not want any inquiries on your credit report that result in denial.

Overdraft Protection

Overdraft protection is a good idea if you live on a tight budget and sometimes get close to a zero balance. It is essentially a line of credit that kicks in if you accidentally write a check for more than the balance of your account. If you do not have overdraft protection and your check bounces, you will be charged a fee by the bank for every check that bounces, and you will start to accumulate negative credit reports in ChexSystems.

To avoid getting into overdraft, you should develop a system for monitoring the level of your account on a daily basis. Whenever you write a check or use your check/debit card, you should have a good idea of how much money is in your account, whether other checks are outstanding that you have not accounted for, and that you have enough money left over to cover this check.

Online banking gives you instant access to the state of your account. You can usually see debit card activity instantly, though it takes a few days for some debit transactions, and for check activity, to be accounted. In any case, it is recommended to write down absolutely everything you spend and keeping complete records so that you are never hit with an unexpected amount from a check you wrote a month ago and had completely forgotten about.

However, just in case that happens, overdraft protection could save you from disaster.

Most lenders will report your overdraft protection to the credit-reporting agencies as a line of credit. If you use it properly — meaning you never use it — it can result in an increase to your FICO score. If you frequently take advantage of your overdraft protection then it might not look so good. You do not want to get in the habit of using your overdraft protection line of credit. Your goal is never to use it. Think of it more as insurance. You purchase homeowner's insurance in case your home burns down, but you hope that it never will, and you do everything you can think of to avoid fires in the home.

Because overdraft protection is a line of credit, you need to qualify for it. Once again, this may not be so easy once the bank sees that bankruptcy on your credit report. They will be a little more lenient if some time has passed — two to three years. Some banks may not qualify you for overdraft protection until your bankruptcy is removed from your credit report. On average, banks will be looking for a FICO credit score of about 680 before granting overdraft protection.

Banks will offer you several different types of overdraft protection. One way is to get a credit card with the bank and tie the bank account to the credit card. If you write a check that is not covered, it is automatically charged to your credit card. You can also tie overdraft protection to a savings account, but you must have money in the savings account for that to work.

If you do not qualify for overdraft protection, a good policy is to keep some amount in your account — say $500 — and plan never to spend it. Then keep good accounting and make sure you never overspend. If there is an error in your calculations and you accidentally write a check that is not covered, you eat into your own $500 account liner and avoid overdraft fees. You must then build back the $500 so that you continue to provide your own protection.

Getting a Checking Account if you are Blacklisted

The easiest way to get a checking account if you have a bad report with ChexSystems is to use a bank that does not use a check-reporting agency.

Use the yellow pages or the Internet to find all the banks in your area. You are especially interested in small and local banks. Call the branch manager and ask him about their different checking account programs. You will want to know the following:

- How much does it take to start an account?

- How long is the approval process?

- Can you be approved online?

- Can you do online banking?

- What check number will they start with?

Next, you can ask how they verify new accounts. Ask them if they review your personal credit report and then ask which credit-reporting agency they use and which check-reporting agency or check-verification service. Make sure you ask about both the credit-reporting agency and the check-verification service — and get answers to both. Ask them which ones they use. If they do not use ChexSystems, you are in luck.

If they do use ChexSystems, you have a couple of choices. You could try to negotiate with them. Tell them that you are listed in ChexSystems and that you can prove you have paid the outstanding amount, because you will have obtained a statement in writing from the bank that reported you. Ask them if there is anything you can do to qualify for an account with them, and then make a note of what they say.

The alternative is to ask them if they know of a local bank that does not use ChexSystems. If they can help you, or refer you to another bank, it could save you some time and frustration. They may be able to tell you about a "fresh start" or "second chance" bank account program that is offered by some banks.

Second-chance bank accounts usually have a probationary period attached to them with limited services for a fixed amount of time — usually six months. After the six months, if your credit is in good standing, and you have managed your account responsibly, you can graduate to a full-service account.

Some banks and credit unions offer courses on how to manage a checking account and require you to pass the course and present a certificate of completion before they will open a checking account for you.

Co-signed Loans

While you are having difficulty being approved for loans, it may be tempting to use a co-signer. If someone with good credit co-signs your loan, you are leveraging their credit worthiness to qualify when you cannot qualify by yourself.

Co-signed loans are rarely a good idea.

Co-signing is not the best way to improve your credit score, and the person who co-signs for you is taking a risk with their own credit score. This type of arrangement frequently leads to unforeseen complications and causes problems for both you and your co-signer. It is much better if you wait until you qualify for a loan on your own merits. This is financially healthier for you and will be better on your financial reports in the end.

Similarly, you should never co-sign a loan for someone else. When you lend someone money you should always be prepared to not get that money back. The same holds true with your credit reputation. When you lend someone your credit reputation, which you do when you co-sign a loan, you should be prepared not to get it back! Can you live with that? On principal, the best thing to do is gently decline if someone wishes you to co-sign on a loan for them.

Here is what happens to the co-signer when the borrower defaults on the loan:

If the loan goes into default, the co-signer must make the payments on the loan.

Each time the loan is 30 days past due, a late payment will appear on the co-signer's credit reports and stay there for seven years. This results in lower FICO scores for the co-signer.

When you use a co-signer to qualify for a loan, the debt-to-income ratio of the co-signer is used in cooperation with the debt-to-income ratio for the borrower. If you are a co-signer on someone else's loan, your personal debt-to-income ratio is now impacted by the other person's debt. That means when you go to qualify for a loan, your borrowing power is now less than it was before. If you were planning on borrowing money for a car or a home before you co-signed the loan, you may not qualify now.

Many credit card companies now systematically increase interest rates when your overall debt ratio rises. This means you could end up having higher interest rates on your currently owned credit cards if you co-sign on someone else's loan.

Increased debt can also affect your ability to get homeowner's insurance or auto insurance or cause your premiums to increase.

There is really no benefit to the co-signer of a loan, and it can have plenty of negative impacts to their own credit.

Co-Signing for Your Children

You might ask yourself if it is acceptable to make an exception to the no-co-signing rule if it is your own children. The truth is, even if your children have never used credit and therefore have no negative credit reporting, there are other ways you can help them to establish credit and obtain financing without having to lay your own credit worthiness on the line.

By not co-signing for them you will be able to help them develop their own good credit habits, and earn their own good credit scores, as well as build a good credit history right from the beginning. Teach them the importance of managing their credit and the value of good credit rating. Teach them to manage money and let them save for a car, a vacation, or whatever it is they want. Children who have grown up depending on your money rapidly develop a new appreciation for its value when they are suddenly called on to earn and spend their own.

Co-Signing With Your Spouse

Your spouse is the only person that it makes sense to co-sign with on a loan. When you are married, your credit and finances are inextricably linked together anyway, and if your spouse has an independent credit history that can bolster your own, that is even better.

However, do not think that just because you are married you automatically need your spouse to co-sign with you. It is always a good idea, even within marriage, to have both joint and independent credit lines. This will set you up for any occurrence and cover all bases, so to speak.

Even if divorce is not in your future, either you or your spouse could become sick or worse, and then the other is left having to survive financially. You will be both be well provided for if you have managed to maintain some degree of financial individuality.

If you are not married, that is a different matter. You have now learned the pitfalls of co-signing, and those are true no matter who you are co-signing with — so be very careful. If you are not sure, you can always pull credit reports for you and your potential co-signer, do a comparison, and look for warning signs.

THE WORLD OF PRIVATE BANKING

Private banks provide financial banking and investment services just like regular banks, but with a more personal touch, and usually for clients who have a least one million dollars in liquid assets. More and more private banks are catering to less wealthy individuals, and sometimes you can find one who will deal with accounts as little as $50,000 or an income of $100,000.

As part of its services, a private bank will help you minimize taxes by advising you on your asset allocation. Many private banks are offshore banks, reducing your tax liability in your country of residence. When we talk about Swiss bank accounts, we are referring to offshore private banking.

Most large banks offer private banking services to a private group of clients. Essentially, it is a unit within the bank where wealthy clients receive a level of service that is quite different from the regular bank clientele.

After you have banked with your private bank for some time, your credit applications are approved without being subject to the usual credit inquiries, reports, and approvals. This is called an "override." Your FICO credit scores can be overridden because of your good standing with your private bank.

Minimum requirements for opening an account with a private bank can range from $100,000 to $250,000. The point here is to motivate you to want to make that kind of salary. As a prior bankrupt person, you are already motivated to get back on track and become financially successful. Why not go all the way?

The thought of having a private banker could be one of the goals that drives you to financial success. Look at your career path and see how it is looking out into the future. Are you on track to increase your salary continually? Are you due for a promotion? Do you have marketable skills you are not fully utilizing? Are you working full-time? Is there anything you could do to start a business on the side? Or moonlight for additional income?

If you are making $100,000 or more a year, or after you do, then call around to banks in your area and find out if they offer private banking services. You may find that you already qualify. The benefit is that the financial nightmare you have been living through could become outdated forever. You could be on track for a completely different sort of life style. It is about creating opportunities for yourself.

Your Insurance Rates After Bankruptcy

Many people do not realize that their insurance rates are affected by their credit scores. A Higher credit score equals lower insurance rates. Additionally, many people do not realize that if their credit score is very low they may be denied insurance altogether. This includes both car and homeowner's insurance.

Your insurance premiums are based on your credit history, including any bankruptcies or collections, defaulted payments, and so on. However, insurance companies do not use FICO scores in the same way that they are used to approve loans. Instead, there are special formulas that are used to calculate your "insurance score." These are what determine whether you qualify for homeowner's or auto insurance. Since they are based on your credit score, your credit score is a good indication for you to determine whether your insurance rates are going to be impacted by your bad credit.

Different states have variations in the rules that govern how insurance companies can use credit scores. For example, Hawaii bans using them altogether for purposes of determining auto insurance, while Pennsylvania and Vermont do not impose any restrictions on using them. Laws in Maryland allow insurance companies to determine rates based on your credit score, but they do not allow them to deny you insurance based on credit scores.

Various other states have variations upon these extremes that fall somewhere in the middle. Some states allow insurance companies to use your credit score in determining whether to approve you for insurance, while others prohibit it. But overall, no matter where you live, you are probably safe enough in making the assumption that your credit score has an impact on your rate.

One way to find out how your rates are calculated in your state is by asking your insurance agent.

Good Credit Lowers Your Insurance Rate

If you have a dispute with your credit report and you think that it has caused your insurance rates to be higher than they otherwise would, you have the right to dispute your credit report, and if you win the dispute, you can notify the insurance company of the resolution. Thirty-six states have laws that require insurance companies to modify your rates within 30 days after you notify them. If you win a dispute and your credit score goes up, insurance companies must adjust your rates accordingly.

The 35 states are: Alabama, Alaska, Arkansas, Colorado,

Connecticut, Delaware, Florida, Georgia, Illinois, Indiana, Iowa, Kansas, Louisiana, Maine, Maryland, Massachusetts, Michigan, Mississippi, Missouri, Nebraska, Nevada, New Hampshire, New York, North Carolina, North Dakota, Ohio, Oklahoma, Oregon, Rhode Island, South Carolina, Tennessee, Texas, Virginia, Washington, and West Virginia.

When you are recovering from bankruptcy, if you notice that your credit scores have risen significantly, you can inform your insurance company and you might be able to get your insurance rate reduced. Remember that they will have to do a credit inquiry, which will have an impact on your score.

YOUR INSURANCE CREDIT SCORE

It might seem unfair that if you are a safe driver and have a pristine driving record, but have missed payments on your credit card, or filed bankruptcy, that your insurance rates should be affected. Once you have filed bankruptcy, your insurance rates could rise dramatically, or even be cancelled, even though you have not had so much as a speeding ticket.

FICO CREDIT SCORES VERSUS INSURANCE CREDIT SCORES

Lenders use your FICO credit score to determine whether you are a good risk for making your payments on time. Insurance companies do not use FICO scores in this way. An insurance company makes its money when you pay your insurance on time and do not file claims. If you file claims, you are not making money for them; they are paying out to you.

Therefore, they are interested in finding out how many claims you make on your insurance and whether they are high- or low-dollar claims.

Your FICO credit score indicates whether you are likely to be a credit-worthy customer who makes your payments on time and repays the money you borrow. Your insurance credit score indicates whether you will be a profitable customer for the insurance company by not making claims. So what is the connection between the two scores? Why are insurance companies interested in your FICO credit score?

Insurance companies believe that there is a relationship between the way you manage money and your likelihood of filing an insurance claim. They have proven that the lower your FICO credit score, the more likely it is that you are going to file insurance claims. In other words, if you are not good at managing money there is a high chance you will file a lot of insurance claims. This means you will not be a profitable customer for the insurance company.

No one has been able to explain why this connection exists. Without solid proof of why the connection exists, there is naturally a lot of controversy surrounding the theory.

The Fair Credit Reporting Act, section 604 allows insurance companies to use your credit score when evaluating your insurance application. The wording spells out explicitly that a credit-reporting agency may provide a credit report if the party inquiring:

"...intends to use the information in connection with the underwriting of insurance involving the consumer."

So, insurance companies are protected by law in the issue of using your credit report to approve your insurance application.

This is probably not good news if you just filed bankruptcy.

KEEPING YOUR INSURANCE RATES LOW

It may not sound logical to you, but in order to keep your insurance rates low you need to keep your credit score as high as possible. The good news is that you already know how to improve your credit scores, because we have examined this through this text. So if you look after your credit score, you are not only increasing your borrowing power and credit worthiness, you are also lowering your insurance rates.

AVOIDING BANKRUPTCY IN THE FIRST PLACE

Bankruptcy, whether Chapter 7 or Chapter 13 (or any of the other chapters), should always be a last resort. Before you and your attorney reach the decision to file, you should explore every possible option to avoid it.

Bankruptcy is often prescribed as a quick-fix solution to

overwhelming financial debt. However, it is far from an easy solution. The road back to financial recovery is long and hard and comes with its own unique set of frustrations. When all is said and done, you are facing about ten years of scarring on your credit report and financial history, along with all the personal embarrassment and shame that comes along with it.

It affects your ability to buy a house, a car, or get employment, and it results in high interest payments and high insurance rates.

After all that, it may not even relieve you of all of your debts, especially if you file under Chapter 13.

Warning Signs

The best way to prevent bankruptcy is to develop good spending habits to begin with. There are some circumstances in which a reversal of financial fortunes can be brought on suddenly by some world event — as happened in Louisiana in the fall of 2005 when Hurricane Katrina devastated entire cities, wiping out businesses in its path — but for the most part, bankruptcies come on slowly as the result of an ever-worsening financial situation. You must be alert for warning signs.

Warning Sign Number 1: Inadequate Medical Insurance

It is hard to know exactly how many bankruptcies are the results of unpaid and overwhelming medical bills. If you or a member of your family experiences a devastating illness and requires prolonged treatment, medical bills can add up fast. Many people are unprotected by medical insurance, and others have extremely high deductibles, high co-pays, and a lifetime cap that is not sufficient to meet bills when something like cancer occurs in the family.

Melissa Jacoby, a law professor at the University of North Carolina, studies the relationship between medical bills and bankruptcy. Jacoby and her colleagues published a study in 1999 showing that more than half a million middle-class families filed bankruptcy following an illness or injury.

Senior citizens with high health bills are especially vulnerable. People have a tendency to max out their credit cards to pay off medical bills or fill their prescriptions and then when the credit card bills come due they do not have the resources to make the payments.

No matter what you think about the state of health care in this country, you need to be aware of the pitfalls and ensure that you and your family have adequate healthcare protection.

Do not just look at the monthly payments and co-pays, but also evaluate the lifetime cap on your medical insurance and make sure it is enough.

If you file for bankruptcy to eliminate your medical debts, your doctors and hospitals are not paid. That means that your chances for receiving continued care from them are reduced. They may decide not to continue treating you if you have not paid their bills.

Warning Sign Number 2: Insufficient Disability Insurance

Often, an unexpected illness will not only rack up high medical bills, but the patient will be unable to work, reducing his income and ability to pay down the bills.

You should have short- and long-term disability insurance. If you have an emergency fund, you may be able to do without short-term disability insurance, but you should absolutely think about long-term disability insurance, especially if you are the sole or primary provider for your family.

Even if you file for bankruptcy and you are able to wipe out most of your medical debts, if there are any ongoing costs associated with the illness — such as prescriptions, periodic scans and X-rays, wheelchair maintenance, and so on — the courts cannot help you with ongoing fees. So if your ability to provide for yourself and your family is impaired, you are going to have difficulty making ends meet a long time after your file for bankruptcy, and your chances for financial recovery decrease.

Warning Sign Number 3: Maxing Out Your Credit Cards

Whether from medical bills or just living beyond your means, if you are regularly up to the spending limit on one or more of your credit cards, you should be worried.

Credit card minimum payment fees are structured to get the maximum possible amount of interest from you, meaning that you pay excessively high prices for anything that you purchase on credit and then do not pay off right away.

If you have been carrying balances on your credit cards and making minimum payments, and yet you continue to use your credit cards, you are headed down a very dangerous path.

There is a very simple solution to high credit card debt. Stop using your credit cards. If you continue to charge items even after you realize that you are having trouble making payments, you need to learn to tell yourself that you simply cannot afford to buy any more "stuff." Just stop charging. Cut up your credit cards and work on paying down your debt.

Warning Sign Number 4: Excessively High Student Loans

We are taught that higher education means higher pay levels, and so we continue to strive to improve ourselves and get more education in the hopes that our incomes will rise. While this is true as a general trend, you need to think carefully before taking out large student loans for higher education.

Think about the salary that you will be able to earn when you graduate and what kind of payment you will be able to afford in order to pay off your student debt. Then ask yourself whether it is worth it to you. If you are studying to become a doctor, chances are you will eventually be making the kind of money that allows you to pay off eight years of medical bills, but it will not be the day you graduate. Every day you do not pay, you are earning more interest on the loan, making it even higher and more difficult to pay off. If you are studying to become a teacher, chances are your salary will not be high enough to pay off the same sort of bills. You will need to borrow less and find other means to pay for your education as you go.

Many times, it is possible to avoid excessively high student loans by taking your degree at a slower pace and paying as you go. You can also consider getting some of your credits at a cheaper establishment such as a community college.

Warning Sign Number 5: Borrowing Against Your Home Equity

If you have borrowed money against the equity in your home, you are depleting a potential source of emergency funding. Some people borrow repeatedly against the equity in their home by refinancing and withdrawing cash. If you are withdrawing the cash against a real financial need, such as a medical emergency, that is one thing. However, if you are withdrawing the cash value in your home so that you can purchase a big-screen TV then you should seriously think twice. Do you really want to use what might be your only resource for emergency funding on a big-screen TV? It is better to wait until you can really afford the TV — chances are that the price will have fallen by then anyway.

Warning Sign Number 6: Insufficient Emergency Fund

An emergency fund is money you set aside for nothing other than emergencies. An emergency is something unprovoked and unanticipated, such as a layoff or an illness that causes you to have sudden expenses beyond your ability to pay for them out of your monthly income.

As a minimum, you should have enough money set aside for three to six months of living expenses as a hedge against unemployment. If you have high medical insurance deductibles, you should have money set aside to cover those too.

Once you start an emergency fund, it should not be used to buy a new car, or a new barbecue grill, or expensive consumer electronics. It is just for emergencies. That way if disaster should ever strike, you will have some resources to fall back on to get you past the worst of it.

DEBT SETTLEMENT OPTIONS

Let us say that you realize you have fallen into the debt trap and you are now in over your head. The first thing you need to do is figure out on paper exactly what your debts are and who you owe. Add up the total amount of debt that you owe. Here are some options that you can consider to pay down the debt.

If the total is less than $50,000, and it is primarily credit card debt, chances are you can work with the credit card companies to come up with a manageable payment plan. You can try to do this by yourself or you can get an attorney to help you. An attorney will most likely be able to work a better plan with the creditors. Most creditors are willing to settle for less, rather than watch you go into bankruptcy and not receive anything at all.

By working with the credit card companies, you may be able to reduce your interest rate and work a lower payment. Some will agree to eliminate the interest altogether if you agree to pay off the entire debt. Others will allow you an extended payment schedule or make some other concession toward the debt to encourage you to pay it off rather than file for bankruptcy.

Another thing you can do is look around your house and figure out what you have that can be sold. Perhaps even the house itself. If you have equity in your house, and you could live in a smaller, cheaper house, then that might be the way to raise capital to pay off excessive credit card debt.

Perhaps you have high car payments and a couple of luxury vehicles sitting in the driveway. You need to ask yourself if you really need to be driving luxury cars while your credit cards are maxed out and you are headed toward financial disaster.

What other assets do you have that could be sold? Exercise equipment that you do not use anymore? Antiques? Jewelry you do not wear anymore or that you can live without? While it might be painful in the short term to sell off things of value that you own, it will be a lot less painful than ten years of recovering from bankruptcy. So be realistic and practical.

Should you use a debt settlement company? In general, these companies take your money and do for you what you could actually do on your own. Rather than spend money on a debt settlement company, you should invest in a good attorney if you do not feel that you can handle matters by yourself.

SELLING YOUR HOME

The thought of selling your home is probably most people's least favorite option. However, if you are sitting on some equity and you are deep in debt, rather than take out a home equity loan, selling your home is another option to consider.

If you take out a home equity loan and use it to pay down your debt you will have two payments. Your original mortgage payment and your equity loan payment. If you sell your home, move into a less expensive home, and use the equity to pay off your debts, you will only have one — hopefully smaller — payment to make. While this hurts in the short term, it might hurt a lot less than foreclosure or bankruptcy. It leaves you in the position of being in control, rather than out of control, and that is worth something.

If you do consider selling your home, you should talk to a tax accountant about capital gains. The laws on capital gains tax have changed over time, so you should definitely find out whether you will be liable for tax on the equity before you decide to sell and find yourself with a sudden and unexpected tax bill.

THE IMPORTANCE OF BUDGETING

Whether or not you have filed bankruptcy — or you are just

reviewing your options at this point — if you are feeling overwhelmed by debt, the best way to begin regaining control is to prepare a detailed budget for yourself.

This is not as hard as it sounds. Budgeting simply means that you write down all your income and balance it against everything you spend. If you are not spending more money than you have coming in, you will be able to manage. We drift toward bankruptcy when minimum payments on our debts exceed our ability to pay for them.

It is recommended that you use a spreadsheet application if you have access to a computer. If not, you can achieve the same thing using a pen and paper and a calculator.

Budgeting is more than just balancing your checkbook. It is about determining how much you can afford to spend on your bills, your life's expenses, and your luxury items, and then staying within that amount. If you know that — after paying all necessary expenses such as your mortgage, your utility bills, and your food — you have X amount of dollars left to play with, then you cannot spend more than that amount.

Knowing how much money you have to spend at any moment in time can prevent you from making rash, spontaneous decisions to acquire luxury items that you cannot afford.

Bouncing Back

So the worst happened: you consolidated your debts and tried to pay them down, but it was just too far beyond your control and you ended up filing bankruptcy.

You can recover from bankruptcy—you can grow financially strong, have good credit scores, and put yourself in the position of never having to be a repeat filer.

But you must learn from your mistakes.

One thing you must learn is good spending habits.

Repeat Filers

Going bankrupt once is bad enough. Going bankrupt twice is usually the result of badly managing your recovery from the initial bankruptcy. Going through it twice does not mean you know what you are doing; it means you have no idea. Clearly you did it wrong the first time; you needed to manage things better.

Repeat filers more than likely got themselves into a position of paying high interest rates on loans that were not discharged, or on new loans that they took out in their attempt to recover from the initial bankruptcy.

It is actually not that easy to refile. There are laws governing how soon you can file for bankruptcy after the first filing. For example, if you file Chapter 7 you must wait eight years before filing Chapter 7 again, and four year before you can file a Chapter 13. If you filed for Chapter 13, you must wait two years before you can file another Chapter 13.

In addition, if you have sufficient assets to file Chapter 13, you will not be allowed to file Chapter 7.

If you have filed for bankruptcy once before, make sure you take time to think about what went wrong and how you can fix it to avoid the need to refile in the future. If you do not improve your spending habits, and learn how to manage your money, you may be setting yourself up to tread the same path twice.

Paying Down Loans That Are Not Discharged

Chances are that even after bankruptcy, you may end up with some loans that have not been discharged. During your bankruptcy filing you will have developed a plan, together with your bankruptcy trustee, to pay off these loans. You will need to be meticulous about making sure all your payments are on time. Whenever you can, pay off more than the minimum. This will not only make the debt disappear faster and reduce the overall interest that you pay, but it will also help your credit score to rebound.

BANKRUPTCY AND YOUR CREDIT CARDS

Many people want to try to hang on to at least one credit card when they file for bankruptcy. Some credit card companies may allow you to hold on to credit cards when you file for bankruptcy, particularly if you do not owe a balance on the card. Others may insist on canceling the card.

Whether or not you are carrying a balance, you will have to declare all your credit cards to your bankruptcy trustee. Your bankruptcy trustee might not allow you to keep the cards.

If you are thinking of keeping a credit card, and you are being allowed to do so by the bankruptcy trustee and by the credit card company, you should seriously think about whether you want to take the risk of having a credit card in your pocket in the first few months following your bankruptcy.

Perhaps it would be better for you psychologically to make a clean start altogether.

SMART FINANCIAL HABITS FOR LIFE

The things you learn about budgeting and managing money during your bankruptcy will hopefully set you up with good habits that you can rely on for the rest of your life. These habits include not buying things you cannot afford, saving up for vacations and major purchases instead of charging them on your credit card, and building an emergency fund and saving it only for emergencies.

There are also other things that you may learn during bankruptcy that will even set you apart from the public, because some people, even though they do not actually go bankrupt, never really learn some of these fundamental skills for maintaining a healthy approach to finances.

Remember to keep an eye on your credit report. You are not just looking to see what your credit scores are, and trying to watch them increase. You are also keeping an eye out on regular basis for warning signs, such as mistakes, and mistaken or stolen identity.

After you are discharged, any debts that have been fully discharged are reported as zero, even if they were not paid off all the way. If your debt has been fully discharged, you do not owe anything on it, nor can your creditor collect on you against that debt. This is the protection you have under the law. Any debts that you had prior to the bankruptcy that were not discharged do not come under the same protection.

It is your responsibility to verify on your credit report that your debts are reported accurately. Make this a lifelong habit.

If you have debts that were not discharged, such as student loans, make sure you always make your payments on time, and do not become delinquent.

If you apply for credit cards, never max them out. Use them only for emergencies, and then make sure you pay them off as soon as you are able. As a rule of thumb, never just make the minimum payments.

You do not need to carry a balance on your credit card in order to build your credit score. Just having one is enough to do that.

Shop wisely for all loans and credit cards. Remember to check your credit scores and work with banks and lenders to find out the terms of the loan and how to qualify. Shop around for the lowest fees and lowest interest rates and do not be afraid to negotiate for better terms.

Very few bankruptcies come on suddenly. Most of the time people build up to them by getting into bad spending habits and letting their debts run away from them. Chances are, therefore, that your credit history was gradually deteriorating for some time before you filed bankruptcy.

Once you have been discharged, and if you have been working at improving your credit score, there is no reason why your credit should not be much more robust following your bankruptcy than it had been for some time prior to the filing.

SUMMARY

People fall upon bankruptcy for all kinds of reasons. Again, everyone's situation is different, so it could have been a number of things that led you to file. Sudden unemployment, broken marriages and divorce, unexpected illness, disability or death, overindulgent use of their credit cards, loans on vehicles they probably should not be driving, or overextending themselves on high mortgage payments are all things that can drive people to the bankruptcy courts to seek relief.

While bankruptcy can seem like an easy way to wipe the slate clean, it is often a long and arduous process to wipe out your debt, clean up your credit history, and get your financial life back under control.

It may be possible to avoid bankruptcy — and you should certainly strive to do so — by consolidating your debts and developing a sound plan for paying them off. Bankruptcy certainly should be a last resort that you turn to only when all your other attempts at financial recovery have failed. If you do choose to file for bankruptcy, you should definitely do so through an attorney to make sure you are fully informed and guided in all aspects of the law and your rights under it.

Nevertheless, recovery following bankruptcy is certainly possible. With a careful strategy and some discipline and patience, you can often be much better off following bankruptcy than you ever were before. It can be a real education in learning how to budget, how to manage money, how to negotiate for the best interest rates, and how to wait for things until you can afford buy them.

Dealing With Bankruptcy

Whether you file for Chapter 13 bankruptcy or whether you file under Chapter 7, your FICO scores are damaged either way. Here are some of the cold, hard facts about filing bankruptcy that you will have to deal with.

If you file under Chapter 13, even though it seems the lesser of two evils because it is not as dramatic, you will still get a black mark on your credit report. Into the bargain, you will be paying off debt for quite a long time. You will be under the financial control of your bankruptcy trustee for three to five years, and will need approval from him or her for every financial move you make. Following that period, you will have to wait another six months for your discharge. That could be five and half years total. During that time, lenders do not treat you any more kindly than they would if you filed under Chapter 7. You are still a bankruptcy case.

From the perspective of your own integrity, you may believe that filing under Chapter 13 is the high road, and filing under Chapter 7 is complete financial ruin. However, consider each situation carefully if you qualify for both. After a Chapter 7 bankruptcy, you can be on your way to financial recovery a long time before you would with a Chapter 13 bankruptcy.

However, the choice is not always yours. The law is written in such a way that if you have any resources to pay off your debts, you are almost forced into filing under Chapter 13 when Chapter 7 would leave you a lot better off. The number-one reason most people file under Chapter 13 is that they have a house to save. Chapter 13 allows you to protect some part of your assets. If your house has a lot of equity this can really be worth it, especially considering what a hard road it is to credit recovery and qualifying for a home loan.

If you do not have a lot of equity, though, it may not make much sense to you to be forced to file under Chapter 13 when you think it would make better sense for you to file for a Chapter 7 bankruptcy.

CREDIT COUNSELING

While there are many good organizations that are genuinely interested in helping you with your debt reduction, there are also many that are trying to make money off of you. Credit counseling is a very good idea in principle, but in reality you need to be very careful about choosing a credit counselor. There are numerous complaints every year about credit counselors that have gouged people who were already financially weakened.

Also be aware that just because an organization says that it is not for profit does not mean that you are going to get the best help from them. The IRS and the Federal Trade Commission have been engaged in cleaning up the credit counseling industry since 2004, and during that time they have dismantled multiple "not-for-profit" organizations.

When you are looking around for help from a credit counselor, do not give out information such as your Social Security number until you are very sure that you are dealing with a reputable organization.

But how do you tell?

Here are some things you can do to make sure you are getting respectable help:

1. Check with local churches and well-known charities to see what help they offer. Often you can get free help locally. Do be aware that although these people may be very nice and willing to help, they are not necessarily qualified financial advisors. This is a good place to start if you are beginning to experience trouble making your payments but you are not in deep water quite yet. If you are definitely in over your head, it may be too late to use this type of resource.

2. It is a good idea to look for a credit counseling organization independently rather than respond to advertisements or television and radio commercials. If you really want to check out one you hear about, use the resources listed in items 3, 4, and 5 below.

3. Many states now require credit counseling agencies to be licensed and registered. You can check on license status and complaints lodged against companies with your state attorney general by checking with the National Association of Attorneys General at **http://www.naag.org**. You can also check with the Better Business Bureau by going to **http://www.bbb.org**. You can also check for complaints with the Federal Trade Commission at **http://www.ftc.gov** and the

independent consumer affairs organization at **http://www.consumeraffairs.com.**

4. You should verify that the credit counseling company you intend to use is registered with the federal trustee program at **http://www.usdoj.gov/ ust/eo/bapcpa/ccde/index.htm.**

5. They should also be listed as a 501 (c) (3) corporation at **http://www.irs.gov**.

6. Ask them about their fees. Not-for-profit agencies should be able to offer you this service without charging a fee. The Trustee Program recommends a fee of no more than $50 for prebankruptcy counseling, and many will waive this fee entirely. However, they may not waive the fee unless you ask about it.

7. Before you sign anything or pay any money, read the contract. You want to understand exactly what they are going to do for you, what service they provide, and what it is going to cost you.

DEBT CONSOLIDATION

Many people ask if they should consolidate their debts so that they just have one easy payment. There are pros and cons to debt consolidation. For example, consolidating all your credit card payments onto a single credit card — pick the one with the lowest interest rate — could be a useful way to attack your debt.

However, beware of being led down the path of taking out a home equity loan to pay off all your credit cards. When you pay for a 30-year mortgage you are paying thousands of dollars in interest. Is this really the way that you want to pay off the pizza you ordered for all your friends after the football game? Or that pair of shoes you just could not resist because they were 70 percent off?

If you bundle all of your debts into your home equity loan and do nothing to improve your spending habits, you may end up with more debt than you started with, only now you get to drag it out for the next 30 years, and you will have lost the benefit of equity in your home as a contingency resource against emergencies.

However, there is one benefit to a home equity loan and that is the fact that the interest you pay on the loan is tax deductible. If your debt is due to a sudden and unexpected emergency — the type that only comes around once in a while, such as a medical condition — then this might be the best way for you to consolidate your payments and get your finances back under control.

There are many resources on the Internet for calculating payments, including tools designed specifically for helping your figure out how much money you will save through debt consolidation. Here are just a couple of resources, but a simple search will reveal many more:

- **http://moneycentral.msn.com/investor/calcs/n_ debt/main.asp**

- **http://www.kiplinger.com/tools**

CONCLUSION

So you have the information in your hands now. The question is, will you go about it the right way? There are no shortcuts that are going to lead you to the same place in a faster time. It is going to take time, and it is going to take effort; it will not be overly easy, but if you do things right from the start, things should be fine.

It is advisable to do things in moderation; do not try to get it all back at once, because it is unrealistic and will only lead to disappointment for you and your loved ones. Baby steps would be a good way to go about it. You need to make a plan and take little steps to get things back where you want them.

Make a plan — a realistic, three-year plan — to get your financial situation back together. In that plan, organize yourself. Buy a calendar and write down the due dates of all your bills, then take one day a week to sit down and pay all your bills for the week. Set up a bank account that will allow you to utilize online bill pay. This will allow you to make payments quickly and pay them all at once, setting the dates for your bank to make the payments.

Another strong recommendation would be to pay half of your payment twice a month. You may be wondering why. There are 52 weeks in a year, and if you make two half-payments each month — say on the 1st and the 15th of the month — you will actually be paying for 13 months instead of 12. This will help lower that balance as well as save you money in interest. Realistically you will not even notice the difference in money; you would have made the full payment that month anyway right? So why not break it up in to two smaller payments and save yourself money over time?

Recovering from bankruptcy is not an easy task, and it is something for which you will need to be mentally strong in order to accomplish. The most important thing is that you stay positive. Brighter days are ahead for you and your family.

BIBLIOGRAPHY

American Bar, Association. *The American Bar Association Guide to Credit and Bankruptcy: Everything You Need to Know About the Law, Your Rights, and Credit, Debt, and Bankruptcy.* Random House Reference, 2006.

Caher, James P., and John M. Caher. *Personal Bankruptcy Laws for Dummies.* For Dummies, 2006.

Lasser, J.K. J.K. *Lasser's the New Bankruptcy Law and You.* Wiley, 2005.

Sitarz, Daniel. Personal Bankruptcy Simplified: *File for Bankruptcy with the New 2005 Bankruptcy Act.* Nova Company, 2006.

Snyder, Stephen. *Credit After Bankruptcy: a Step-by-Step Action Plan to Quick and Lasting Recovery After Personal Bankruptcy.* Bellwether Publications, 2005.

http://www.Equifax.com
http://www.Experian.com
http://www.fightidentitytheft.com/credit_bureaus.html
http://www.TransUnion.com
https://www.consumerdebit.com/consumerinfo/us/en/index.htm
http://www.ftc.gov/bcp/menus/consumer/credit.shtm

AUTHOR BIOGRAPHY

Mitch Wakem was born and raised in New England. After obtaining his degree in business management and a successful career in numerous sales positions, he turned his knowledge to writing.

Mitch writes mostly business related books and articles, but has more recently focused on some comical self-help books.

Mitch currently lives in South West Georgia.

INDEX